Daily MATH 4 Practice

The premise behind *Daily Math Practice* is simple and straightforward—frequent, focused practice leads to mastery and retention of the skills practiced.

Daily Math Practice is based on current NCTM standards and is designed to support any curriculum that you may be using in your classroom.

What's in *Daily Math Practice*?

◆ The book is divided into 36 weekly sections.

◆ Monday through Thursday follow this format:

    • two computation problems

    During the first 18 weeks the computation problems are organized with addition on Monday, subtraction on Tuesday, multiplication on Wednesday, and division on Thursday.

    During the second 18 weeks (weeks 19–36) the computation problems are presented in random order.

    • two items that practice a variety of math skills

    • one word problem

◆ Friday's format includes one problem that is more extensive and may require multiple steps. These problems emphasize reasoning and communication in mathematics.

◆ An answer key for each week is provided on the same page as the Friday lesson.

◆ Scope and sequence charts on pages 3 and 4 detail the specific skills to be practiced and show when they will be presented. Computation is not listed as a specific skill because it is addressed every day in *Daily Math Practice*.

About the Author:

Wes Tuttle began his teaching career as a junior high mathematics teacher in California. After completing a Master's Degree in Gifted Education at the University of Northern Colorado, Wes coordinated the gifted program and taught at Christa McAuliffe Elementary School in Greeley, Colorado. He served as the school's Teacher on Special Assignment developing curriculum guidelines and monitoring compliance with state and national standards. He is currently completing his Doctorate in Educational Leadership, directing and teaching in a Summer Enrichment Program for gifted students, and coordinating math curriculum development and delivery at a district level.

Author: Wes Tuttle
Editor: Marilyn Evans
Copy Editor: Cathy Harber
Desktop: Carolina Caird
Cover Design: Cheryl Puckett

Entire contents ©1999 by EVAN-MOOR CORP.
18 Lower Ragsdale Drive, Monterey, CA 93940-5746.
Permission is hereby granted to the individual purchaser to reproduce student materials in this book for noncommercial individual or classroom use only. Permission is not granted for schoolwide, or systemwide, reproduction of materials.
Printed in U.S.A.

EMC 753

How to Use *Daily Math Practice*

You may want to use all of the following presentations throughout the year to keep each lesson fresh and interesting.

1. Make overhead transparencies of the lessons. Present each lesson as an oral activity with the entire class. Write answers and make corrections using an erasable marker.

   As the class becomes more familiar with *Daily Math Practice*, you may want students to mark their answers first and then check them against correct responses marked on the transparency.

2. Reproduce the pages for individuals or partners to work on independently. Check answers as a group, using an overhead transparency to model the correct answers. (Use these pages as independent practice only after much oral group experience with the lessons.)

3. Occasionally you may want to use a day's or even a full week's lesson(s) as a test to see how individuals are progressing in their acquisition of skills.

Some Important Considerations

1. Allow students to use whatever tools they need to solve problems. Some students will choose to use manipulatives, while others will want to make drawings.

2. It is important that students be able to share their solutions. This modeling of a variety of problem-solving techniques provides a great learning benefit. Don't scrimp on the amount of time you allow for discussing how solutions were reached.

3. With the focus of the first four days being on computation and problem solving, it is recommended that calculators be used only on Fridays, when the focus is much more detailed, with less emphasis on computation. In some instances, however, you may want to allow the use of calculators to solve the daily word problems.

Suggestions and Options

1. Sometimes you will not have taught a given skill before it appears in a lesson. These items should then be done together. Tell the class that you are going to work on a skill they have not yet been taught. Use the practice time to conduct a minilesson on that skill.

2. Customize the daily lessons to the needs of your class.

   - If there are skills that are not included in the grade-level expectancies of the particular program you teach, you may choose to skip those items.

   - If you feel your class needs more practice than is provided, add these "extras" on your own in the form of a one-item warm-up or posttest.

3. Many of the Friday problems are quite challenging and lend themselves to partner or small-group collaboration.

Skills Scope & Sequence

Week	1	2	3	4	5	6	7	8	9	10	11	12	13	14	15	16	17	18	19	20	21	22	23	24	25	26	27	28	29	30	31	32	33	34	35	36
Numbers																																				
base-ten system	●		●		●	●	●			●						●						●	●						●			●	●			●
word/standard forms				●				●												●				●				●				●				
place value							●							●			●		●	●			●				●				●				●	
rounding		●					●																		●		●						●			
odd/even numbers			●					●				●										●							●					●		
ordinals				●		●																									●					
estimation									●						●					●	●					●								●		
properties/number relationships										●				●			●			●	●			●			●					●				
factors	●		●					●				●					●								●				●					●		
multiples					●				●					●					●		●			●				●	●			●				●
inequalities	●						●											●	●			●			●					●					●	
decimals			●	●	●						●					●					●				●											
fractions		●		●	●			●									●					●				●					●			●	●	
Patterns/Algebra																																				
figural patterns			●		●	●	●	●	●			●				●	●		●	●			●	●				●	●				●			
numerical patterns	●					●	●				●				●		●		●				●				●			●		●				●
expressions				●		●			●				●				●			●					●		●		●					●		
function tables						●					●	●				●	●					●											●			
ratios			●	●				●				●					●				●				●					●	●		●			
Geometry/Spatial																																				
2-dimensional shapes	●		●					●	●		●		●			●					●		●		●		●		●		●	●	●			
3-dimensional shapes		●	●										●	●	●					●								●					●			
congruency						●				●								●		●						●				●				●	●	
symmetry				●										●	●				●						●		●		●							●
spatial			●						●						●			●	●			●							●		●					
angles													●													●							●			

Week	1	2	3	4	5	6	7	8	9	10	11	12	13	14	15	16	17	18	19	20	21	22	23	24	25	26	27	28	29	30	31	32	33	34	35	36
Measurement																																				
length	•				•			•					•					•	•	•				•					•		•	•			•	
weight		•	•		•					•				•		•			•				•					•						•		
capacity			•				•		•		•	•					•					•			•	•	•			•					•	•
time			•		•	•			•		•	•	•	•	•	•	•			•				•	•	•	•	•			•			•	•	•
temperature									•					•						•		•				•					•					•
money	•	•	•		•	•		•	•	•	•	•		•	•		•	•		•		•	•	•	•	•	•	•	•	•		•	•	•		•
perimeter		•				•			•		•				•				•					•				•								•
area						•						•				•					•					•					•					•
volume							•						•					•							•					•					•	
calendar				•						•				•	•			•							•			•						•		
Data/Probability																																				
coordinate graphing					•					•						•					•						•						•			
number lines							•					•						•	•				•							•					•	
constructing graphs		•	•	•				•					•						•					•					•		•	•			•	
interpreting graphs								•								•									•			•	•			•			•	
range	•							•										•													•					
mode				•		•								•													•									
median		•				•																•														
probability		•				•					•				•					•						•					•					•
permutations/combinations					•					•		•						•								•									•	

©1999 by Evan-Moor Corp.

4

Daily Math Practice, Grade 4 • EMC 753

Name:

1. 8
      +2

2. 14 + 25 = _____

3. Write everything you can about what makes a figure a square.

_____

_____

_____

_____

4. What is 10 tens equal to?

_____

5. Sally was walking to school and noticed that she walked past 16 houses along the way. If each house has two dogs, how many dogs would Sally walk past on her way to school?

_____

Name:

1. 15
      − 6

2. 52 − 41 = _____

3. What polygon has six sides?

_____

4. What is the range of these numbers?

15, 18, 19, 23, 25

_____

5. Jimmy and Alex are each collecting baseball cards. Between them, they have 128 cards. If Jimmy has 72, how many does Alex have?

_____

Daily Math Practice, Grade 4 • EMC 753

Name: _____

1. $\begin{array}{r} 5 \\ \times\ 8 \\ \hline \end{array}$

2. $2 \times 9 =$ _____

3. Which is longer, 10 centimeters or 12 inches?

_____

4. What place value does the 4 have in 4,093?

_____

5. Ben has six cats. If he gives three of them away, how many will he have left?

_____

Name: _____

1. $3\overline{)15}$

2. $28 \div 4 =$ _____

3. Fill in the correct symbol.

$< = >$

$37 \bigcirc 68$

4. What are the next three numbers in this pattern?

7, 12, 17, 22, ____, ____, ____

5. Jennifer is collecting money to buy a new CD. The CD costs $14.00. If she has $8.00, how much more money does she need?

_____

Use the figure below and the following clues to solve this problem. Notice that each section of the figure is labeled with a letter. Your task is to find out what whole number goes in each region and what color it should be.

1. The number in the red section is twice as much as the number in the B section.
2. The blue section is 5.
3. The smallest number is in the green section.
4. The sum of the numbers in A and C is 13.
5. The only prime number is in A.

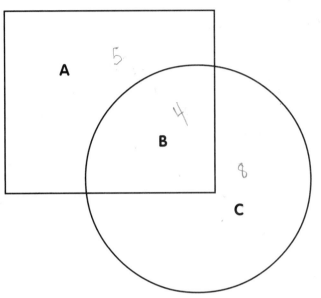

MATH ①
Practice

Answer Key

Monday

1. 10
2. 39
3. A square is a polygon that has four sides that are equal in length. It also has four angles that are right angles with 90 degrees each. The sum of the angles in a square is 360 degrees.
4. 100
5. 32 dogs

Tuesday

1. 9
2. 11
3. hexagon
4. 10
5. Alex has 56 baseball cards.

Wednesday

1. 40
2. 18
3. 12 inches
4. thousands
5. 3 cats

Thursday

1. 5
2. 7
3. < (less than)
4. 27, 32, 37
5. $6.00

Friday

A–5–blue, B–4–green, C–8–red

1.   5
   + 9

2. 14 + 39 = _____

3. Construct a graph for this information. Use a piece of graph paper or the back of this page.

Favorite Drink	Number of Students
soda	16
milk	8
water	10
juice	5

4. What temperature does this thermometer read?

_____

30
20
10

5. Greg and Juan were earning money by collecting newspapers to recycle. They agreed to evenly split the total money earned. The first day Greg collected $2.00 and Juan collected $1.50. The second day Greg collected $1.75 and Juan collected $3.25. Once the money was totaled and divided evenly, how much money did each boy receive?

_____

1.   9
   − 5

2. 26 − 12 = _____

3. If Sam has six red socks and five blue socks in his dresser drawer, what is the probability he will pull out a red one in the dark?

_____

4. Round 369 to the nearest hundred.

_____

5. Cathy is two years older than Wendy. Wendy is eight years old. How old will Cathy be in two years?

_____

1.   4
      x 1

2. 9 x 5 = _____

3. What solid figure has congruent squares on all six sides?

_____

4. What fraction of this box is shaded?

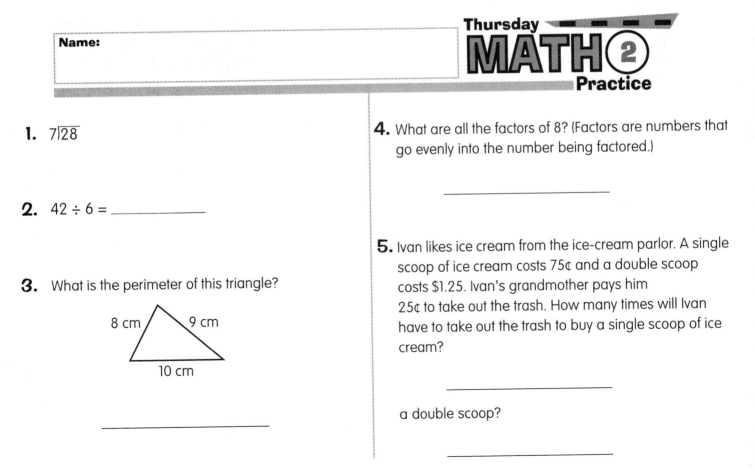

_____

5. Vanessa collects baseball cards. She has thirty-six in her current collection. If her brother gives her two for her birthday, her mother gives her three for Christmas, and her uncle gives her his collection of fourteen cards, how many cards will Vanessa own?

_____

1. 7)28

2. 42 ÷ 6 = _____

3. What is the perimeter of this triangle?

8 cm   9 cm

10 cm

_____

4. What are all the factors of 8? (Factors are numbers that go evenly into the number being factored.)

_____

5. Ivan likes ice cream from the ice-cream parlor. A single scoop of ice cream costs 75¢ and a double scoop costs $1.25. Ivan's grandmother pays him 25¢ to take out the trash. How many times will Ivan have to take out the trash to buy a single scoop of ice cream?

_____

a double scoop?

_____

Name: _____

Louisa and her three friends were making a pizza for lunch. They wanted to share the pizza evenly and couldn't decide whether they should use a rectangular-shaped pan or a circular-shaped pan. Show different ways to cut the pizza using these rectangles and circles. Shade in Louisa's piece and write what portion of the pizza she is going to get.

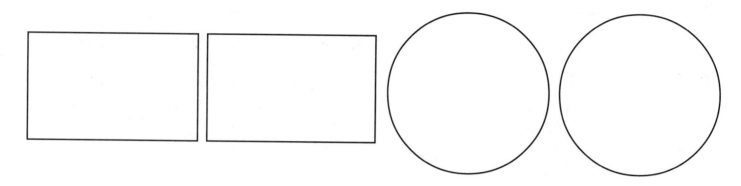

Answer Key

Monday

1. 14
2. 53
3.

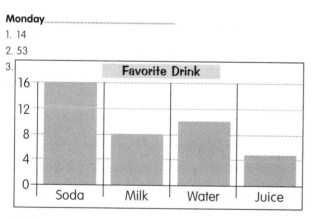

4. 22 degrees
5. $4.25

Tuesday

1. 4
2. 14
3. 6 out of 11 or $\frac{6}{11}$
4. 400
5. 12 years old

Wednesday

1. 4
2. 45
3. a cube
4. $\frac{2}{3}$
5. 55 cards

Thursday

1. 4
2. 7
3. 27 cm
4. 1, 2, 4, and 8
5. single scoop = 3 times, double scoop = 5 times

Friday

Many possible answers are available for the division of the pans, including the following:

Louisa's portion is always one-fourth or $\frac{1}{4}$.

1.   6
      + 2

2. 53 + 74 = _____

3. How many blocks are in this figure? _____

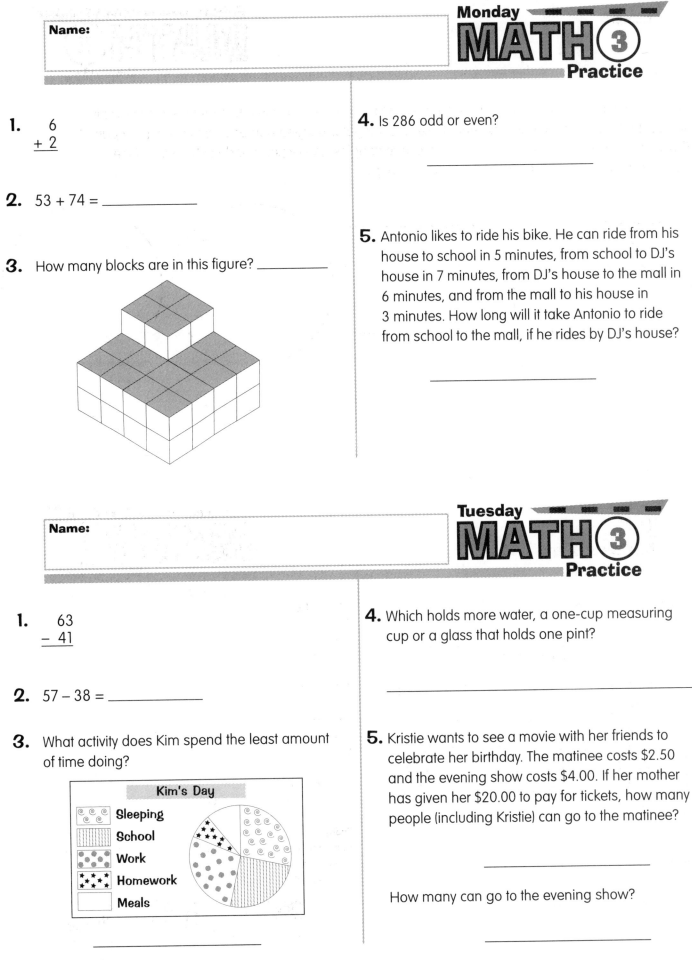

4. Is 286 odd or even?

_____

5. Antonio likes to ride his bike. He can ride from his house to school in 5 minutes, from school to DJ's house in 7 minutes, from DJ's house to the mall in 6 minutes, and from the mall to his house in 3 minutes. How long will it take Antonio to ride from school to the mall, if he rides by DJ's house?

_____

1.   63
      – 41

2. 57 – 38 = _____

3. What activity does Kim spend the least amount of time doing?

Kim's Day
- Sleeping
- School
- Work
- Homework
- Meals

_____

4. Which holds more water, a one-cup measuring cup or a glass that holds one pint?

_____

5. Kristie wants to see a movie with her friends to celebrate her birthday. The matinee costs $2.50 and the evening show costs $4.00. If her mother has given her $20.00 to pay for tickets, how many people (including Kristie) can go to the matinee?

_____

How many can go to the evening show?

Daily Math Practice, Grade 4 • EMC 753

1. $\begin{array}{r} 2 \\ \times\ 5 \\ \hline \end{array}$

2. $7 \times 0 =$ _____

3. What comes next in this pattern?

△ △ ⊘ ⊘ △ △ ⊘ ___

4. Which of these are NOT trapezoids?

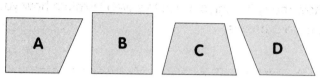

A   B   C   D

_____

5. Yolanda's cat had six kittens. After choosing one kitten for herself, Yolanda decided to sell the remaining kittens for three dollars each. If she sold all of the remaining kittens, how much money would Yolanda have made?

_____

---

1. $2\overline{)4}$

2. $48 \div 8 =$ _____

3. According to this graph, 2 Gerails correspond to how many Yellatails?

```
14
12 |\
10 | \
 8 |  \
 6 |   \___
 4 |       \___
 2 |           _____
 0 |_____
   2  4  6  8 10 12 14 16 18
          Yellatails
```
(Gerails)

_____

4. Which is larger, 0.8 or 2?

_____

5. Marcos is 48 inches tall. His younger brother, Carlos, is 7 inches shorter than Marcos. Marcos's older brother, Raul, is 13 inches taller than Carlos. How tall is Raul?

_____

Name:

Even though you can't see the whole spider web, how many triangles are in this web? Explain how you got your answer.

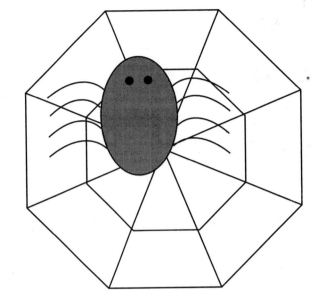

_____

_____

_____

_____

Answer Key

Monday
1. 8
2. 127
3. 36
4. even
5. 13 minutes

Tuesday
1. 22
2. 19
3. homework
4. the glass that holds one pint
5. matinee = 8 people, evening = 5 people

Wednesday
1. 10
2. 0
3. ∅
4. B and D
5. $15

Thursday
1. 2
2. 6
3. 10 Yellatails
4. 2
5. Raul is 54 inches tall (4 feet, 6 inches).

Friday
16 triangles, because there are 8 small triangles and 8 larger triangles.

1.   212
     + 510

2. 392 + 586 = _____

3. What is a good estimate for 11 times 351?

_____

4. Given this figure, write the ratio for the number of shaded boxes compared to the total number of boxes.

_____

5. Kurt collects marbles. Half of his marbles are green, 3 are red, 4 are blue, and the rest are white. If Kurt has 28 marbles altogether, how many white marbles does he have?

_____

1.   365
     − 143

2. 855 − 746 = _____

3. If March 1st is on Thursday, what day of the week does March 23rd fall on?

March						
Sun.	Mon.	Tues.	Wed.	Thurs.	Fri.	Sat.

_____

4. Write this number in standard form.

two hundred sixty-three

_____

5. Sylvia has several gerbils. If one of her gerbils has 6 babies every two months, how many baby gerbils will it have over one year's time?

_____

1.   6
     x 4

2. 3 x 6 = _____

3. Explain what 0.1 means.

_____

_____

_____

4. If $M = 2$, then what does $M + 3$ equal?

_____

5. Ted's car will go 25 miles on each gallon of gas. His tank holds 10 gallons of gas when it is full. If Ted wants to take a 700-mile trip, and he starts with a full tank of gas, what is the minimum number of times he will need to stop for gas?

_____

1. 2)‾18‾

2. 15 ÷ 5 = _____

3. How many blocks are in this figure?

_____

4. What is the mode (most frequently appearing item) of this data?

25, 27, 29, 30, 30, 31, 34, 35, 37, 39

_____

5. Andrea owns a video game system. She owns 27 games, and she's played them all many times. There is a store in town that will trade three used games for one new one. If Andrea trades in all of her current games, how many new games will she receive?

_____

The Venn diagram below shows multiples of two different numbers. All the numbers are less than 50. The center section is left blank. These numbers are called "common multiples."

Which common multiples should go here?

_____

How do you know?

_____

_____

_____

_____

_____

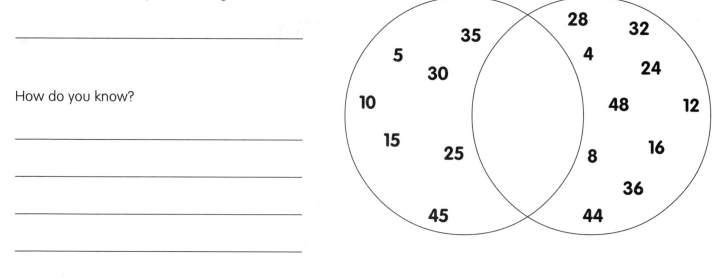

MATH ④
Practice

Answer Key

1. 638
      + 347

2. 165 + 881 = _____

3. How many different ways can 3 kids line up for lunch?

      _____

4. If this is a cm ruler, how long is this rocket?

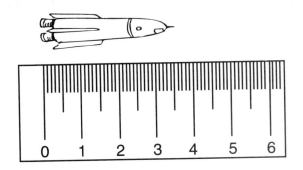

0   1   2   3   4   5   6

5. Kiko likes to fish. She caught an 8 pound 3 ounce trout in Blue Mountain Lake. The record catch so far that season was 129 ounces. Since 16 ounces equals a pound, did Kiko's fish beat the record?

      _____

1. 458
      − 129

2. 842 − 157 = _____

3. What are the coordinates of **X** on this graph?

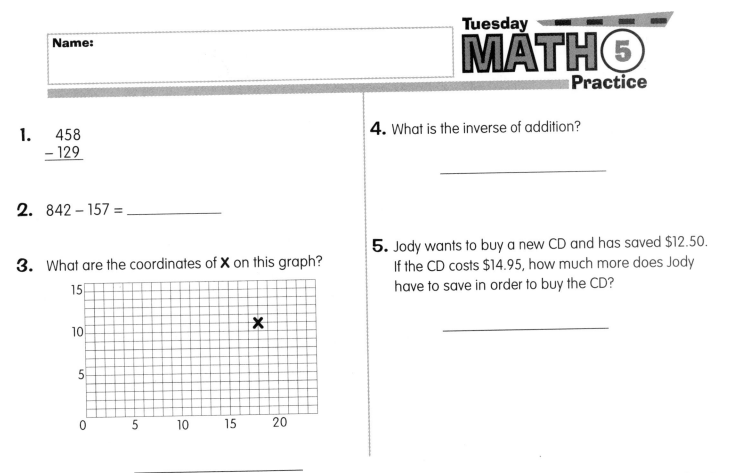

15

10

5

0   5   10   15   20

      _____

4. What is the inverse of addition?

      _____

5. Jody wants to buy a new CD and has saved $12.50. If the CD costs $14.95, how much more does Jody have to save in order to buy the CD?

      _____

1.   8
     x 8

2. 1 x 7 = _____

3. What decimal represents the amount of shading in this figure?

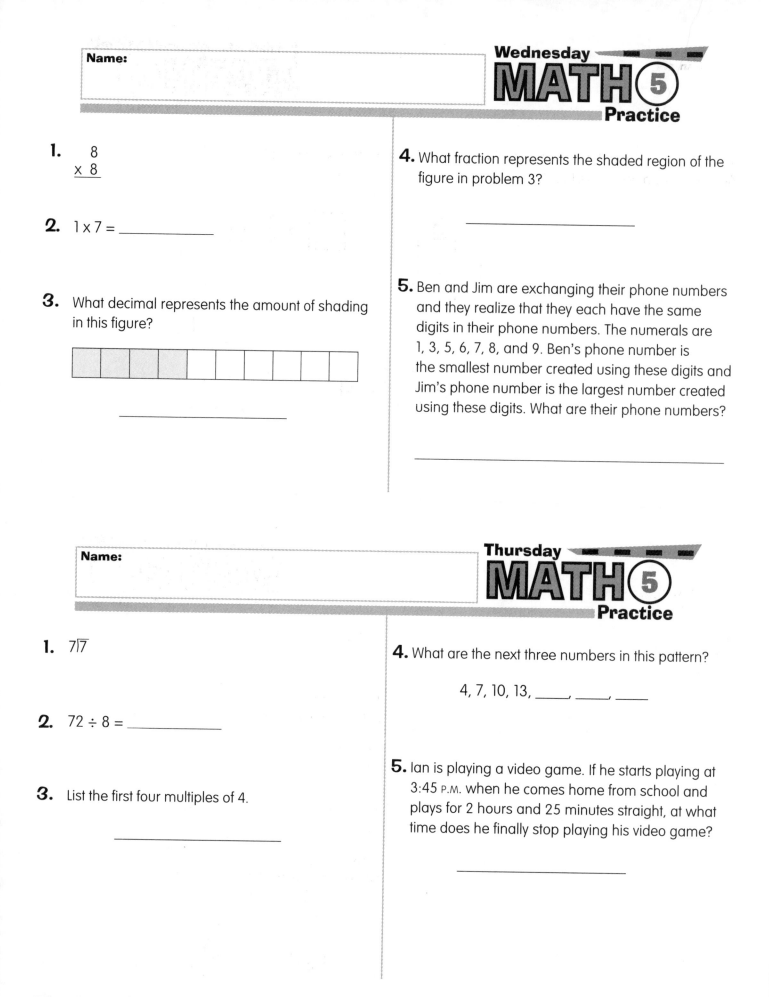

_____

4. What fraction represents the shaded region of the figure in problem 3?

_____

5. Ben and Jim are exchanging their phone numbers and they realize that they each have the same digits in their phone numbers. The numerals are 1, 3, 5, 6, 7, 8, and 9. Ben's phone number is the smallest number created using these digits and Jim's phone number is the largest number created using these digits. What are their phone numbers?

_____

1. 7⟌7

2. 72 ÷ 8 = _____

3. List the first four multiples of 4.

_____

4. What are the next three numbers in this pattern?

4, 7, 10, 13, _____, _____, _____

5. Ian is playing a video game. If he starts playing at 3:45 P.M. when he comes home from school and plays for 2 hours and 25 minutes straight, at what time does he finally stop playing his video game?

_____

Name:

Use the digits 1 through 9 to complete these number sentences. Use each digit only once.
Are there any other possible solutions?

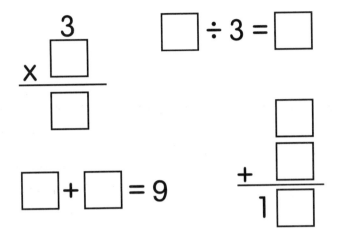

Answer Key

MATH ⑤

Practice

Monday
1. 985
2. 1,046
3. 6
4. 3.6 cm or 36 mm
5. Yes, because Kiko's fish was 131 ounces.

Tuesday
1. 329
2. 685
3. (18, 11)
4. subtraction
5. $2.45

Wednesday
1. 64
2. 7
3. 0.4
4. $\frac{4}{10}$ (could be reduced to $\frac{2}{5}$)
5. Jim's phone number is 987-6531 and Ben's phone number is 135-6789.

Thursday
1. 1
2. 9
3. 4, 8, 12, 16
4. 16, 19, 22
5. 6:10 P.M.

Friday
There are many possible solutions. One solution is:

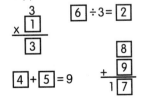

1.   584
       + 392

2.   467 + 232 = _____

3.   What is the area of this shape if each square represents 1 inch by 1 inch?

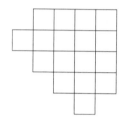

_____

4. What is the perimeter of the shape in problem 3?

_____

5. Brandon has a stack of books sitting on his desk. The first one has 10 pages, the next one has twice as many pages, 20 pages. The next one has twice as many pages again, or 40 pages. This pattern continues for eight books. How many pages are in the eighth book?

_____

1.   738
       − 295

2.   197 − 126 = _____

3. What is the median (or middle value) of this data?

        10, 12, 13, 14, 16, 17, 19

_____

4. What is the eighth letter in this question, not counting spaces? (W is the first, h is the second, etc.)

_____

5. Abby is half as old as her dad, but twice as old as her brother Scott. If Scott is 9, how old is their dad?

_____

1.   7
      x 6

2. 2 x 2 = _____

3. Complete this function table if 2 is **added to each** input to get the output.

Input	4	6	8	
Output	6	8	10	12

4. Does this shape have at least one line of symmetry? If so, how many?

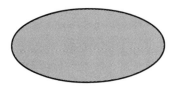

_____

5. Rafael can run one mile in 8 minutes. If he keeps this rate up, how long will it take him to run 5 miles?

_____

---

1. 9⟌18

2. 25 ÷ 5 = _____

3. What is 20 tens equal to?

_____

4. What figure comes next in this pattern?

_____

5. Maria is selling T-shirts for her school's Student Council. Each shirt sells for $8, and the school keeps half of that as profit. If Maria sells 12 shirts, how much money has she earned for the school's Student Council?

_____

Given this spinner and the following rules, tell if this is a fair game. If so, explain why you think it is fair. If not, explain why not and who has a better chance of winning.

Rules:
1. You take turns spinning the spinner.
2. If it lands on the white region, you get a point.
3. If it lands on the shaded region, the other person gets a point.
4. The first person to get 20 points wins.

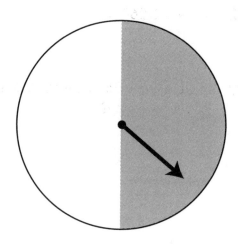

_____

_____

_____

_____

MATH ⑥
Practice

Answer Key

Monday
1. 976
2. 699
3. 17 square inches
4. 20 inches
5. 1,280 pages

Tuesday
1. 443
2. 71
3. 14
4. h
5. 36 years old

Wednesday
1. 42
2. 4
3. 10
4. yes, two
5. 40 minutes

Thursday
1. 2
2. 5
3. 200
4.
5. $48

Friday
It is a fair game because both regions are half of the circle, so they each have the same chance of being spun each time.

Name:

1.   285
     + 206

2. 4,719 + 5,260 = _____

3. In the number 26,195, what digit is in the thousands place?

_____

4. Which letter represents 4 on this number line?

_____

5. Louise and Frank are each collecting baseball cards. If Louise has three times as many cards as Frank and she has 84, how many cards does Frank have?

_____

Name:

1.   743
     − 551

2. 6,328 − 5,104 = _____

3. Fill in the correct symbol.

< = >

36 ◯ 24

4. Give three examples of items that have the same shape as a rectangular prism.

_____

_____

_____

5. Tim has just set up his 10-gallon fish tank in his bedroom. He has 10 neon tetras, 8 guppies, and 3 blue gouramis in his aquarium. How many fish does he have in all?

_____

Daily Math Practice, Grade 4 • EMC 753

1. 10
　　 x 7

2. 1 x 4 = _____

3. Round 275,390 to the nearest ten-thousand.

_____

4. What is the volume of this cube?

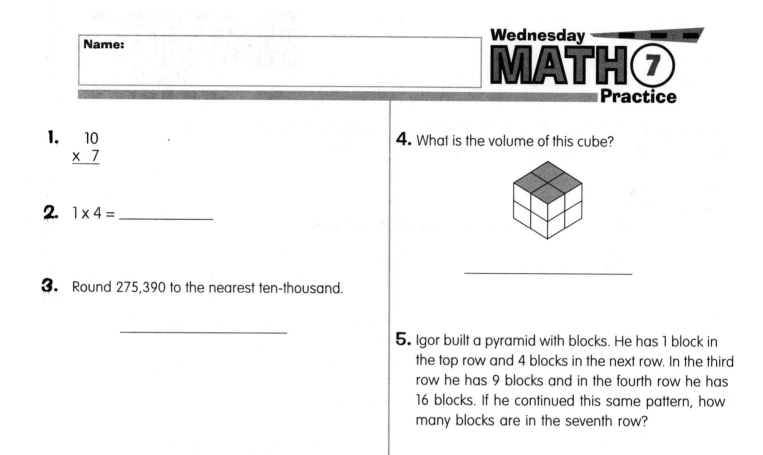

_____

5. Igor built a pyramid with blocks. He has 1 block in the top row and 4 blocks in the next row. In the third row he has 9 blocks and in the fourth row he has 16 blocks. If he continued this same pattern, how many blocks are in the seventh row?

_____

1. 5)‾40‾

2. 40 ÷ 10 = _____

3. How many quarts are in a gallon?

_____

4. What number is represented by this model?

_____

5. Matt has 2 pet mice. Eric has 3 pet birds. Kirstin has 4 pet hamsters. If each pet eats one-quarter cup of food each day, how much food do they need altogether for 8 days?

_____

　　　24　　　Daily Math Practice, Grade 4 • EMC 753

Sam, George, and Kelley each have a different last name. Use this grid and the list of clues to determine who has what pet and what each person's full name is.

1. The Smith's daughter has a cat.
2. Sam is short for Samantha.
3. No letters from the child's first name appear in the child's last name.
4. The Kin's son has a pet rabbit.
5. The Kipler's child has a pet snake.

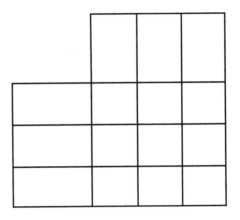

MATH ⑦
Practice

Answer Key

Monday
1. 491
2. 9,979
3. 6
4. B
5. 28 baseball cards

Tuesday
1. 192
2. 1,224
3. > (more than)
4. There are many possible answers, including: file cabinet, box of tissues, box of cereal, CD case, etc.
5. 21 fish

Wednesday
1. 70
2. 4
3. 280,000
4. 8 cubic units
5. 49 blocks

Thursday
1. 8
2. 4
3. 4
4. 135
5. 18 cups of food

Friday
Sam (Samantha) Kipler has a snake, George Kin has a rabbit, and Kelley Smith has a cat.

	cat	rabbit	snake
Smith	Kelley	X	X
Kin	X	George	X
Kipler	X	X	Sam

Name:

1. 7,243
+1,609

2. 3,857 + 2,691 = _____

3. What is the range of this data?

36, 64, 37, 45, 53, 60

_____

4. What figure should replace the question mark?

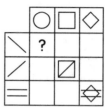

_____

5. Min is three times as tall as her brother. If Min is 5 feet, 3 inches tall, how tall is her brother?

_____

Name:

1. 2,608
−1,427

2. 6,847 − 5,963 = _____

3. Write the number 539 in word form.

_____

4. List all the factors of 10.

_____

5. Dave is walking home from school and is attempting not to step on any of the cracks in the sidewalk. He finds that there are 15 cracks in front of each house and there are 12 houses that he walks past. How many cracks are there in all that Dave needs to try not to step on?

_____

Name: _____

1.   0
      x 6

2. 5 x 5 = _____

3. Is 841 odd or even?

_____

4. What fraction does the shaded part represent?

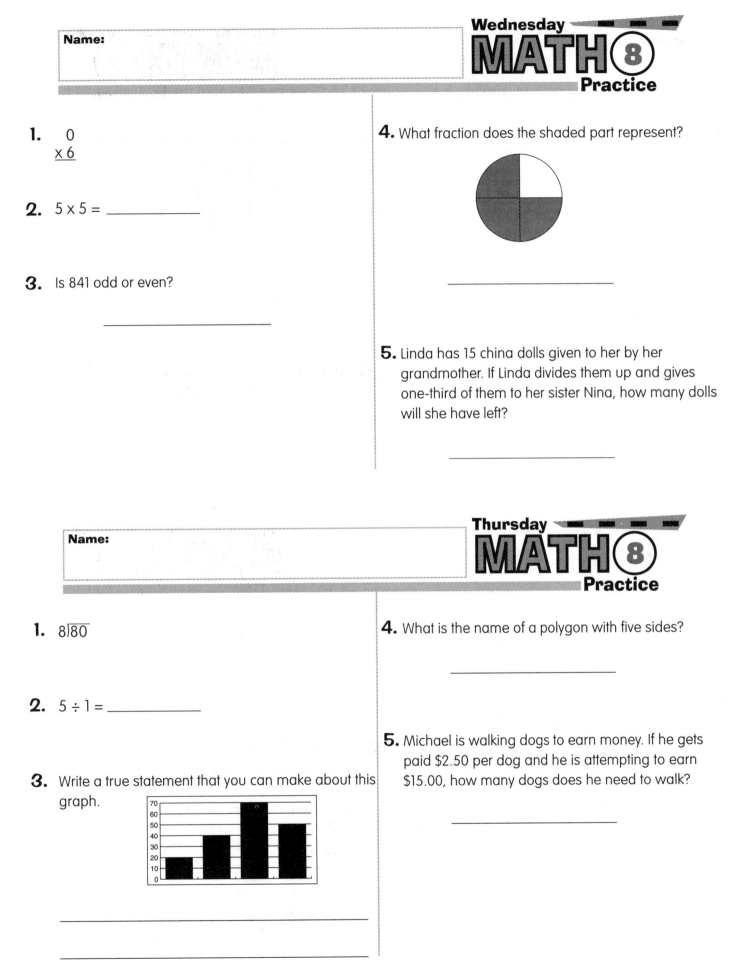

_____

5. Linda has 15 china dolls given to her by her grandmother. If Linda divides them up and gives one-third of them to her sister Nina, how many dolls will she have left?

_____

Name: _____

1. 8)‾80‾

2. 5 ÷ 1 = _____

3. Write a true statement that you can make about this graph.

_____

_____

4. What is the name of a polygon with five sides?

_____

5. Michael is walking dogs to earn money. If he gets paid $2.50 per dog and he is attempting to earn $15.00, how many dogs does he need to walk?

_____

Tyler read 8 books, Rose read 6 books, Brett read 5 books, and Suzy read 12 books. Use this data to make a graph. Use a piece of graph paper or the back of this page. Then write three questions that could be answered using this graph and answer the questions.

_____

_____

_____

_____

_____

MATH ⑧
Practice

Answer Key

Monday
1. 8,852
2. 6,548
3. 28
4. ⊘
5. 21 inches or 1 foot, 9 inches

Tuesday
1. 1,181
2. 884
3. five hundred thirty-nine
4. 1, 2, 5, and 10
5. 180 cracks

Wednesday
1. 0
2. 25
3. odd
4. $\frac{3}{4}$
5. 10 china dolls

Thursday
1. 10
2. 5
3. There are many possible answers, including:
   The range of the data is 50.
   The most popular one had 70 requests/votes.
   The tallest bar was over three times more than the shortest bar.
   The fewest people liked the first item.
4. pentagon
5. 6 dogs

Friday
Many possible questions and graphs can be created, including:
Who read the most books? Suzy; How many books did they read in all? 31;
How many more books did Tyler read than Brett? 3

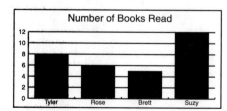

1. 275
+ 368

2. 4,751 + 3,126 = _____

3. Is 4 a good estimate for 158 ÷ 41? Why or why not?

_____

_____

_____

4. List the first three multiples of 6.

_____

5. Jesse was starting a collection of stamps. When he began, his grandfather gave him 48 stamps. Then his parents gave him 23 stamps and his aunt gave him 17 stamps. How many stamps does Jesse now have in his collection?

_____

1. 7,264
– 3,758

2. 6,479 – 5,432 = _____

3. What time does this clock show?

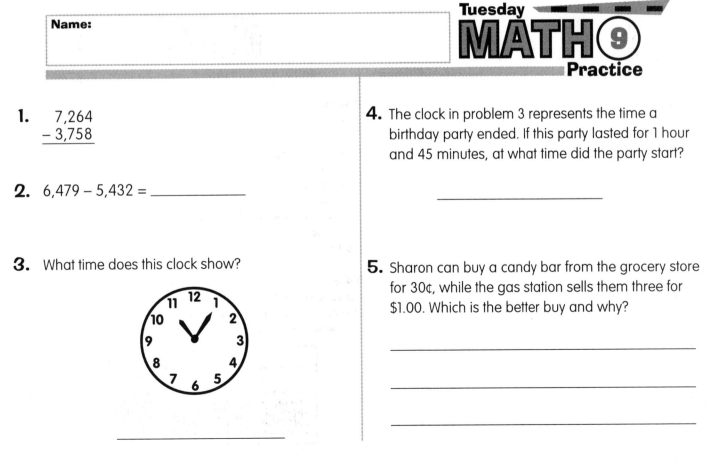

4. The clock in problem 3 represents the time a birthday party ended. If this party lasted for 1 hour and 45 minutes, at what time did the party start?

_____

5. Sharon can buy a candy bar from the grocery store for 30¢, while the gas station sells them three for $1.00. Which is the better buy and why?

_____

_____

_____

1. 0
x 10

2. 8 x 4 = _____

3. Which of these figures is NOT a polygon?

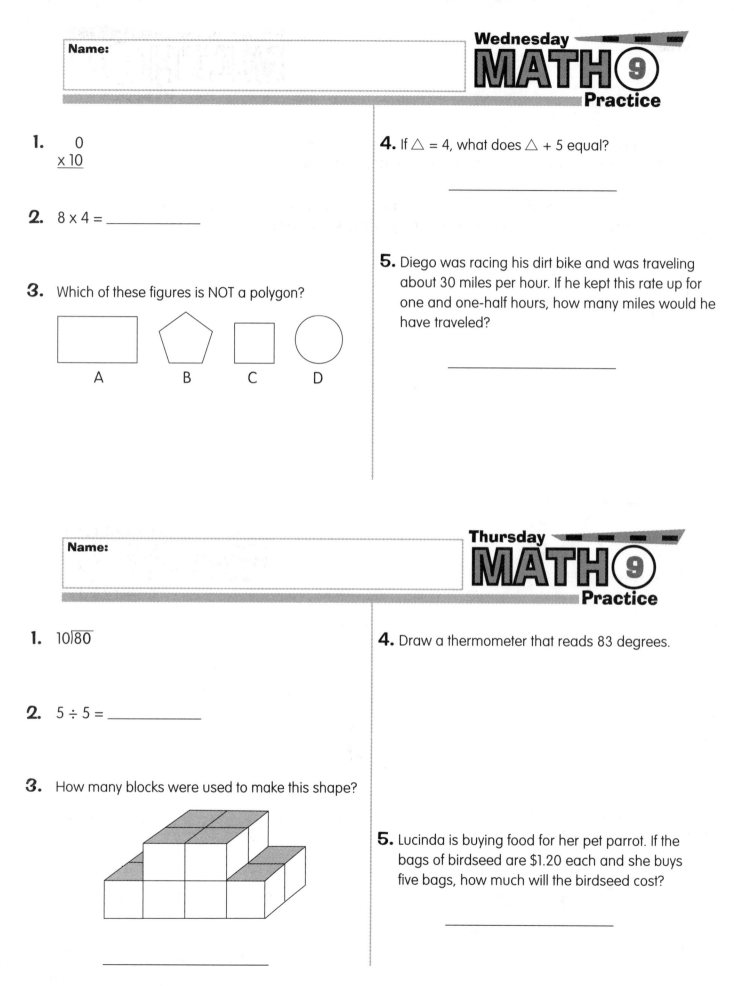

A   B   C   D

4. If △ = 4, what does △ + 5 equal?

_____

5. Diego was racing his dirt bike and was traveling about 30 miles per hour. If he kept this rate up for one and one-half hours, how many miles would he have traveled?

_____

1. 10⟌80

2. 5 ÷ 5 = _____

3. How many blocks were used to make this shape?

_____

4. Draw a thermometer that reads 83 degrees.

5. Lucinda is buying food for her pet parrot. If the bags of birdseed are $1.20 each and she buys five bags, how much will the birdseed cost?

_____

If you take 4 squares that are all one inch by one inch and place them side by side, you will have a figure that has an area of 4 square inches. The perimeter of this shape will be 10 inches.

How many different ways can you arrange these 4 squares if they have to be joined along an edge and not just at the corners? What is the perimeter of each of these figures?

Answer Key

Monday
1. 643
2. 7,877
3. Yes, because 160 divided by 40 is equal to 4.
4. 6, 12, and 18
5. 88 stamps

Tuesday
1. 3,506
2. 1,047
3. 11:05
4. 9:20
5. The grocery store is the better buy, because she can buy three candy bars there for only 90¢.

Wednesday
1. 0
2. 32
3. D
4. 9
5. 45 miles

Thursday
1. 8
2. 1
3. 12 blocks
4. There are many possible answers, including:

5. $6.00

Friday
There are seven possible arrangements. (Students may have additional ones that are rotated from one of these.)

Perimeter = 8"   Perimeter = 10"   Perimeter = 10"   Perimeter = 10"

Perimeter = 10"   Perimeter = 10"   Perimeter = 10"

1. 7,951
   +1,368

2. 187 + 247 = _____

3. Ten hundreds is equal to what?

_____

4. What is the inverse of multiplication?

_____

5. Karl jogs with his father every morning. Saturdays they run 4 miles and on all other days they run 2 miles. How many miles does Karl run each week?

_____

---

1. 6,245
   – 3,816

2. 227 – 199 = _____

3. How many lines of symmetry does this shape have?

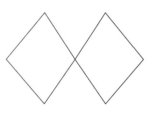

_____

4. Ramon has three dimes, six nickels, and seven pennies. How much money does he have?

_____

5. Jenny can type 30 words per minute. How many words can she type in 5 minutes?

_____

1. 4
   x 7

2. 9 x 2 = _____

3. Hallie is washing the dishes and putting them away after dinner. As she puts them into the cupboard, she can put a maximum of 4 bowls in each stack. If she has 18 bowls to put away, what is the minimum number of stacks Hallie will have?

_____

4. Plot the point (5, 12) on this graph.

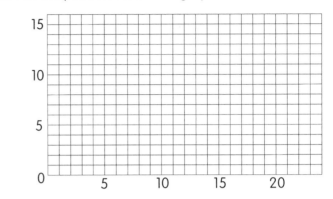

5. Which is heavier, one pound of rocks or one pound of feathers?

_____

1. 4)24

2. 14 ÷ 7 = _____

3. How many different ways can Athena put together 3 different blouses and 3 different pairs of pants?

_____

4. What month comes 4 months after April?

_____

5. Mario is going to an amusement park on Saturday. The park charges 50¢ per ride, and Mario wants to ride all 19 rides at least once. What is the minimum amount of money he should bring?

_____

Brian is thinking of a number and gives these clues:

    1. It is less than 50.

    2. It is not a multiple of 5.

    3. It is odd.

    4. It is greater than 20.

    5. It has a 3 in the ones place.

Brian still has not given enough information to figure out his number. What numbers could he

be thinking of? _____

Choose one of these numbers and write another clue that will help someone narrow in on your number.

_____

_____

MATH (10)
Practice

Answer Key

Monday

1. 9,319
2. 434
3. 1,000
4. division
5. 16 miles

Tuesday

1. 2,429
2. 28
3. 2
4. 67¢ or $0.67
5. 150 words

Wednesday

1. 28
2. 18
3. 5 stacks
4.

5. They weigh the same; they are both one pound.

Thursday

1. 6   4. August
2. 2   5. $9.50
3. 9

Friday

Brian could be thinking of 23, 33, or 43. Students' clues will vary depending on which number they select. An example for 33 might be "The numeral in the tens place is the same as the ones place."

1.   387
       + 523

2. 4,725 + 3,626 = _____

3. What is the perimeter of this shape if each square is 1 inch by 1 inch?

_____

4. What is the next number in this pattern?

5, 9, 13, 17, _____

5. Holly reaches in her pocket and realizes that she has 33¢. What are three different combinations of coins that she could have?

_____

_____

_____

---

1.   931
       − 642

2. 7,109 − 5,423 = _____

3. If there are 3 red marbles and 2 blue marbles in a bag, what is the probability that you will pick out a red one with your eyes shut?

_____

4. Approximately what time does this clock show?

_____

5. John has two more dogs than he has chickens. If he has 8 dogs, how many chickens does he have?

_____

1.   10
      x 6

2. 9 x 7 = _____

3. Name three items that have the same shape as a cylinder.

_____

_____

_____

4. What decimal represents the shaded part of this figure?

_____

5. During the soccer season, Rosa scored at least one point during half of her games. If she played 8 games, in how many games did Rosa score?

_____

1. 9⟌45

2. 50 ÷ 5 = _____

3. Complete this input/output chart.

Input	8	10	12	14
Output	2	4		8

4. In problem 3, what is the rule for the chart?

_____

5. April is baking muffins for breakfast. Each box makes 8 muffins, and she needs 27 muffins. How many boxes does April need to use?

_____

There are 97 fourth grade students in Scott Elementary School. They are planning to go to the zoo on a field trip. In addition to the students, 4 teachers and 10 parents are going as well. The zoo charges $1.00 for each student and $2.00 for each adult. It costs the school $150.00 for each bus.

If each bus holds 45 people, how many buses will be needed?

_____

How much money will the school have to pay for the buses and the zoo entrance costs?

_____

Answer Key

Monday
1. 910
2. 8,351
3. 20 inches
4. 21
5. There are many possible answers, including:
   1 quarter, 1 nickel, and 3 pennies
   3 dimes and 3 pennies
   33 pennies

Tuesday
1. 289
2. 1,686
3. 3 out of 5 or $\frac{3}{5}$
4. about 7:28
5. 6 chickens

Wednesday
1. 60
2. 63
3. There are many possible answers, including: soup can, trash can, drinking glass, pencil, roll of paper towels, etc.
4. 0.5
5. 4 games

Thursday
1. 5
2. 10
3. 6
4. The output is the input minus 6.
5. 4 boxes

Friday
They will need 3 buses. The costs will be $450.00 for the buses, $97.00 for the students' entrance fees, and $28.00 for the adults' entrance fees. The total cost will be $575.00.

Name:

1.   3,846
      + 5,152

2.   638 + 271 = _____

3.   How many cups are in a quart?

      _____

4. Mark an **X** on this number line to show 2.7.

5. Sal is playing with four other friends in his backyard. They are jumping on the trampoline, but the trampoline will hold only two people at a time. If each friend wants to jump with each of the others, how many turns altogether do they need to take?

      _____

Name:

1.   9,496
      − 7,391

2.   279 − 183 = _____

3.   Round 3,948 to the nearest hundred.

      _____

4. List all the factors of 9.

      _____

5. Susan is bird watching and sees 3 beautiful birds on Monday. On Tuesday she sees 4 more. On Wednesday she sees 6 and on Thursday she doesn't see any. Then on Friday, she sees 4 again. How many birds did Susan see during the week, assuming that each bird sighting was of a different bird?

      _____

1.   10
     x 4

2. 6 x 1 = _____

3. Is 49 odd or even?

_____

4. What figure is next in this pattern?

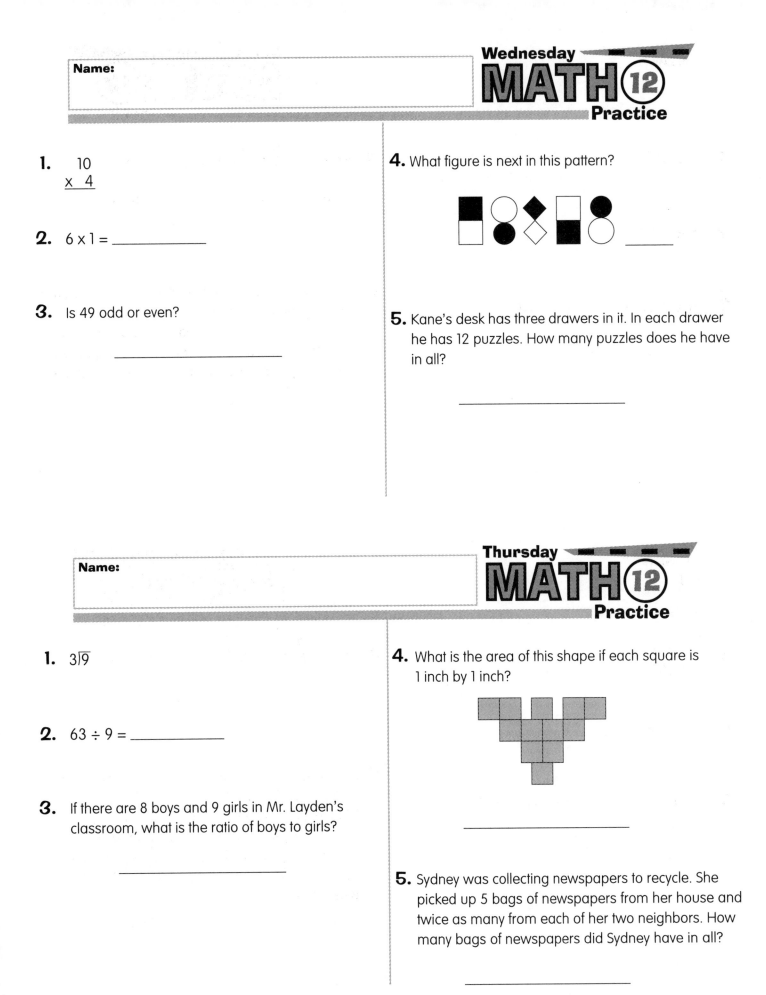

_____

5. Kane's desk has three drawers in it. In each drawer he has 12 puzzles. How many puzzles does he have in all?

_____

1. 3)‾9

2. 63 ÷ 9 = _____

3. If there are 8 boys and 9 girls in Mr. Layden's classroom, what is the ratio of boys to girls?

_____

4. What is the area of this shape if each square is 1 inch by 1 inch?

_____

5. Sydney was collecting newspapers to recycle. She picked up 5 bags of newspapers from her house and twice as many from each of her two neighbors. How many bags of newspapers did Sydney have in all?

_____

At 11:11 the digits on a digital clock are all the same. At what other times does this happen? The time 11:11 can also be read in reverse order and still be 11:11.

What other times can be read in reverse order and still be the same? (Be careful, 9:09 doesn't work because of where the colon would lie. It would be 90:9 reversed.)

_____

_____

_____

MATH ⑫
Practice

Answer Key

Monday
1. 8,998
2. 909
3. 4
4.
5. 10 turns

Tuesday
1. 2,105
2. 96
3. 3,900
4. 1, 3, and 9
5. 17 birds

Wednesday
1. 40
2. 6
3. odd
4. ◆
5. 36 puzzles

Thursday
1. 3
2. 7
3. 8 to 9 or 8:9
4. 12 square inches
5. 25 bags of newspapers

Friday
The digits are the same at 1:11, 2:22, 3:33, 4:44, 5:55, and the given 11:11.

The times the clock can be read in reverse and still be the same are 10:01, 12:21, and the given 11:11.

Name:

1.   405
     + 360

2. 3,154 + 5,918 = _____

3. How many feet are in 3 yards?

_____

4. What is the volume of this prism?

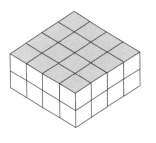

_____

5. If a pyramid with a square base is set on top of a cube and exactly covers the top, how many faces will the shape have on the outside?

_____

Name:

1.   857
     − 142

2. 3,684 − 1,792 = _____

3. Write this number in standard notation.

two hundred fifty-three

_____

4. What is half of 24?

_____

5. Mara has 6 fewer stuffed animals than her sister Sarah. If Sarah has 23 stuffed animals, how many does Mara have?

_____

1.   2
    x 8

2.   10 x 3 = _____

3.   If $w = 7$, then what does $w - 3$ equal?

   _____

4. What is the name of a triangle that has two sides that are the same length?

   _____

5. Tonya was drawing pictures on the back of her homework papers. It took her about 5 minutes to draw each picture. This week alone, she turned in 18 assignments with her drawings on them. How long did it take Tonya to draw the 18 drawings?

   _____

---

1.   8)‾40‾

2.   9 ÷ 9 = _____

3. Construct a graph to represent this information. Use a piece of graph paper or the back of this page.

Month	Average Temperature
January	39
February	46
March	53
April	69
May	82
June	95

4. Fill in the correct symbol.

   < = >

   8.4 ◯ 14

5. Webster was cleaning his room and found 57 books under his bed. He put them in stacks with the same number of books in each stack (1 book by itself does not count as a stack). How many stacks did he make?

   _____

Mona needs to catch 12 grasshoppers to feed to her pet snake. She figures it takes her about 3 minutes to catch each one. If there is one-half hour before her school bus comes to pick her up, does she have enough time to catch all the grasshoppers she needs? Explain why or why not.

_____

_____

_____

_____

MATH ⑬
Practice

Answer Key

Monday
1. 765
2. 9,072
3. 9 feet
4. 32 cubic units
5. 9 faces

Tuesday
1. 715
2. 1,892
3. 253
4. 12
5. 17 stuffed animals

Wednesday
1. 16
2. 30
3. 4
4. isosceles triangle
5. 90 minutes or $1\frac{1}{2}$ hours

Thursday
1. 5
2. 1
3. One possible graph:

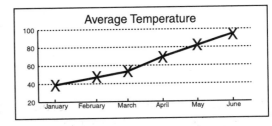

4. < (less than)
5. 3 stacks or 19 stacks

Friday
No, she does not have enough time because it would take her about 36 minutes to catch the grasshoppers, and she only has 30 minutes before the bus comes to pick her up.

1. 3,251
 + 4,806

2. 317 + 394 = _____

3. What place value does the 5 have in 53,890?

 _____

4. Estimate the value of 890 + 201.

 _____

5. Nathan is saving money to buy a new shirt that costs $24.00. He currently has $15.00. How much more does Nathan need to save?

 _____

1. 7,243
 − 5,612

2. 204 − 148 = _____

3. What are the first four multiples of 7?

 _____

4. Which figure fits in the white space?

A   B   C   D

5. Julie has a pet dog that eats 3 cups of food each day. If the bag of dog food contains enough food for 35 days, how many cups of food are in the bag?

 _____

1.   4
     x 4

2. 8 x 7 = _____

3. What temperature is 23 degrees above freezing in Fahrenheit?

_____

4. If February 1st is on a Friday, what day will the 21st fall on?

February						
Sun.	Mon.	Tues.	Wed.	Thurs.	Fri.	Sat.

_____

5. Amy is buying five bags of chips and each one costs $1.25. What will be the total cost of the chips?

_____

1. 6)̄36

2. 54 ÷ 6 = _____

3. What is the mode (most frequently appearing item) of this data?

26, 29, 30, 31, 31, 35, 35, 35, 36, 39, 40

_____

4. How many pounds are equal to 128 ounces?

_____

5. Suppose that you are facing north. Each time you turn, you are going to turn 90 degrees. If you turn 2 times to the right, 1 time to the left, 3 times to the right, 2 times to the right, and 1 time to the left, which way are you now facing?

_____

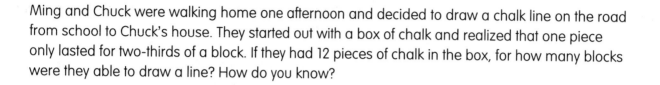
Ming and Chuck were walking home one afternoon and decided to draw a chalk line on the road from school to Chuck's house. They started out with a box of chalk and realized that one piece only lasted for two-thirds of a block. If they had 12 pieces of chalk in the box, for how many blocks were they able to draw a line? How do you know?

_____

_____

_____

MATH ⑭

Practice

Answer Key

Monday

1. 8,057
2. 711
3. ten-thousands
4. The actual value is 1,091. Students' answers will vary, including 1,100 or 1,090, for example.
5. $9

Tuesday

1. 1,631
2. 56
3. 7, 14, 21, and 28
4. A
5. 105 cups

Wednesday

1. 16
2. 56
3. 55 degrees
4. Thursday
5. $6.25

Thursday

1. 6
2. 9
3. 35
4. 8 pounds
5. east

Friday

For 8 blocks, because it took 3 pieces of chalk to draw a line for 2 blocks. If they had 12 pieces of chalk, they could do that 4 times. Then, 4 times 2 blocks is 8 blocks that they could draw the line.

Name:

1.   4,233
    + 4,698

2. 540 + 279 = _____

3. What is 3 hours and 15 minutes after 2:55 A.M.?

    _____

4. What is the probability of spinning a 2 on this spinner?

    _____

5. Anna is swinging on the swings during recess. She can swing back and forth 22 times each minute. If the recess is 15 minutes long, how many times can Anna swing back and forth?

    _____

Name:

1.   7,346
    – 5,627

2. 174 – 158 = _____

3. In terms of dollars, how much is 5,000 pennies worth?

    _____

4. What is the inverse of subtraction?

    _____

5. Kendall is going to dance lessons every Tuesday afternoon. About how many times does she go each month?

    _____

1. $\begin{array}{r} 5 \\ \times 2 \\ \hline \end{array}$

2. $7 \times 8 =$ _____

3. What are the next three numbers in this pattern?

2, 4, 8, 16, _____, _____, _____

4. How many faces does this pyramid have?

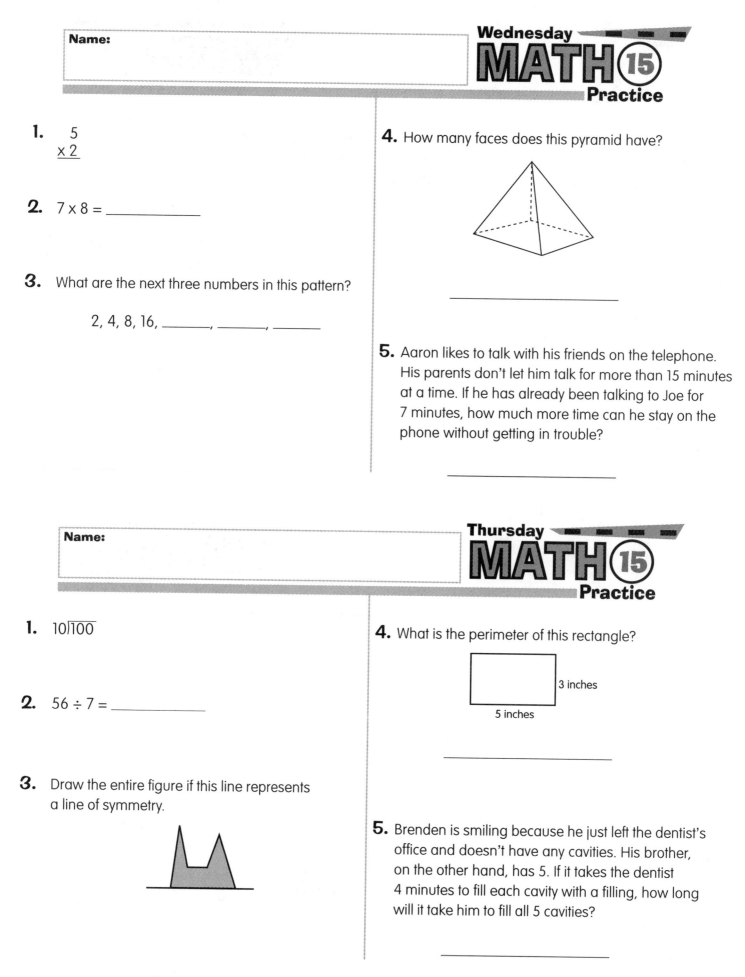

_____

5. Aaron likes to talk with his friends on the telephone. His parents don't let him talk for more than 15 minutes at a time. If he has already been talking to Joe for 7 minutes, how much more time can he stay on the phone without getting in trouble?

_____

1. $10\overline{)100}$

2. $56 \div 7 =$ _____

3. Draw the entire figure if this line represents a line of symmetry.

4. What is the perimeter of this rectangle?

3 inches

5 inches

_____

5. Brenden is smiling because he just left the dentist's office and doesn't have any cavities. His brother, on the other hand, has 5. If it takes the dentist 4 minutes to fill each cavity with a filling, how long will it take him to fill all 5 cavities?

_____

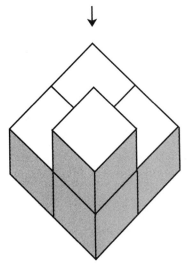

Draw what this building would look like if you were standing on the opposite side of the building, looking at it from where the arrow is pointing. Assume that all four sides of each block are gray and all the tops are white.

MATH 15
Practice

Answer Key

Monday

1. 8,931
2. 819
3. 6:10 A.M.
4. 1 out of 2 or $\frac{1}{2}$
5. 330 times

Tuesday

1. 1,719
2. 16
3. 50 dollars
4. addition
5. either 4 or 5, depending on the month

Wednesday

1. 10
2. 56
3. 32, 64, 128
4. 5 faces
5. 8 more minutes

Thursday

1. 10
2. 8
3.
4. 16 inches
5. 20 minutes

Friday

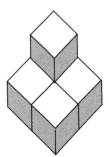

1.   349
        + 375

2. 4,806 + 2,223 = _____

3. What are the coordinates of point **X** on this graph?

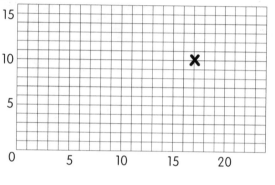

_____

4. Round 369 to the nearest ten.

_____

5. Shelby is doing her homework and discovers that it takes her about 3 minutes to do each math problem. If she has 18 problems left to do, about how long will it take her to finish her homework?

_____

---

1.   756
        − 369

2. 6,438 − 2,905 = _____

3. What is the area of this shape if each square is 1 square centimeter?

_____

4. What polygon has 5 straight edges?

_____

5. Andy is the kicker for his football team. During Saturday's game he kicked three field goals for three points each, then the team scored 2 touchdowns (6 points each), and they also got the extra point for each touchdown (1 more point each). The other team scored a total of 20 points. Did Andy's team win the game?

_____

Name: _____

1. $\begin{array}{r} 9 \\ \times\, 9 \\ \hline \end{array}$

2. $7 \times 5 =$ _____

3. If the rule for this input/output function is to add 3, fill in the missing spaces.

Input	3	5	9		20
Output	6		12	21	

4. What does 10 hundred thousands equal?

_____

5. Luke was fishing with his dad and caught a fish that was 2 pounds and 4 ounces. If each pound is equal to 16 ounces, how many ounces did Luke's fish weigh?

_____

Name: _____

1. $6\overline{)24}$

2. $12 \div 2 =$ _____

3. Given this graph, who has the most items altogether?

4. Using the graph in problem 3, how many more pens does Gwen have than Nadia?

_____

5. Shannon was raking leaves in her front yard. She figured it would take 12 bags to hold the leaves from 2 trees. If Shannon has 7 trees (each the same size), how many bags would she need to hold all the leaves?

_____

         Daily Math Practice, Grade 4 • EMC 753

Start with the square on the left and divide it into fourths. The last figure shows this division being done one more time, dividing each square into fourths again. If you did this two more times, how many squares would you have? Justify your answer.

 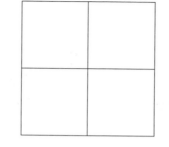 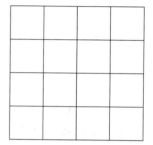

Answer Key

MATH 16
Practice

Monday
1. 724
2. 7,029
3. (17, 10)
4. 370
5. about 54 minutes

Tuesday
1. 387
2. 3,533
3. 7 square centimeters
4. pentagon
5. Yes they won, because Andy's team scored 23 points and the other team only scored 20 points.

Wednesday
1. 81
2. 35
3.

Input	3	5	9	18	20
Output	6	8	12	21	23

4. 1 million or 1,000,000
5. 36 ounces

Thursday
1. 4
2. 6
3. Ruth
4. 4 more pens
5. 42 bags

Friday
There would be 256 squares, because each time you are multiplying the number of squares in the previous figure by 4. You had 16 squares and you multiply that by 4 and get 64. Then 64 times 4 equals 256.

1.   3,869
      + 4,902

2. 379 + 620 = _____

3. Write the number three hundred thousand
       sixty-eight in standard form.

       _____

4. List all the factors of 20.

       _____

5. Marcy was in a pie eating contest. She was
       able to eat 3 cream pies that each contained
       15 cherries. How many cherries did she eat in all?

       _____

1.   3,428
      − 1,965

2. 637 − 214 = _____

3. Is 794 odd or even?

       _____

4. If 6 people want Todd Smith for their class
       president and 17 people want Toni Johnson,
       what is the ratio of people wanting Todd to the
       people wanting Toni for class president?

       _____

5. Elizabeth was going on a flight with her family.
       The plane left the airport at 10:15 A.M. She was
       served lunch 42 minutes into the flight. If it took
       her 13 minutes to eat her lunch, at what time did
       Elizabeth finish eating?

       _____

Name: _____

1. 3
    x 4
    ───

2. 6 × 9 = _____

3. What decimal represents the shaded portion of this circle?

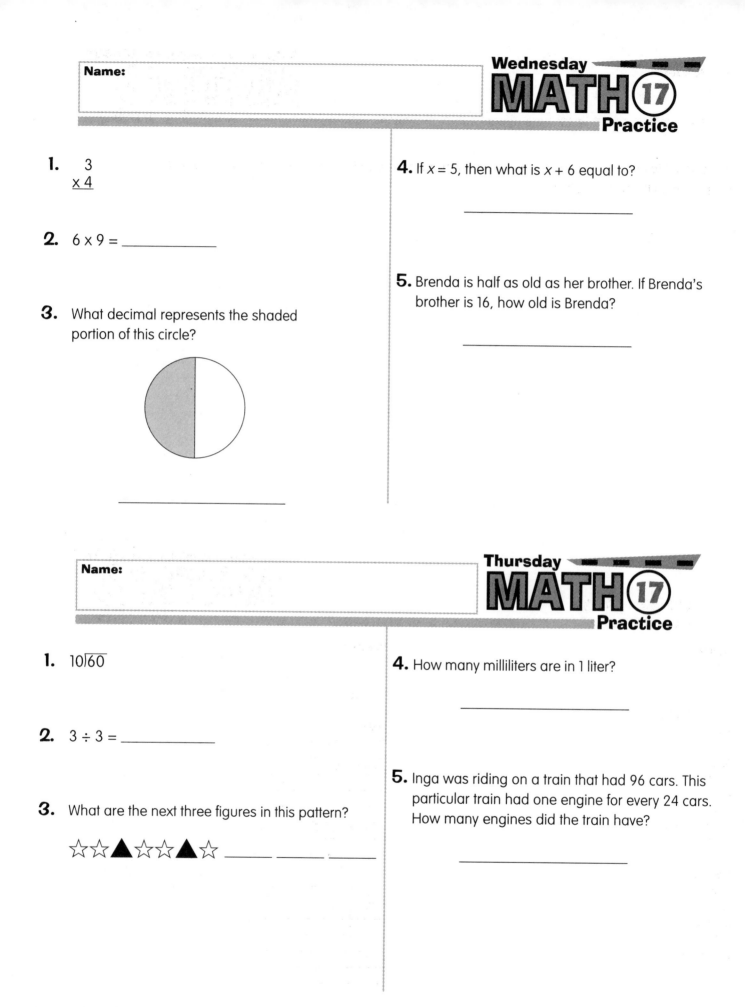

_____

4. If $x = 5$, then what is $x + 6$ equal to?

_____

5. Brenda is half as old as her brother. If Brenda's brother is 16, how old is Brenda?

_____

Name: _____

1. 10)‾60‾

2. 3 ÷ 3 = _____

3. What are the next three figures in this pattern?

☆☆▲☆☆▲☆ _____ _____ _____

4. How many milliliters are in 1 liter?

_____

5. Inga was riding on a train that had 96 cars. This particular train had one engine for every 24 cars. How many engines did the train have?

_____

Anton has 27¢ in his pocket. How many different possible combinations of coins could he have? Make of list of these possibilities.

Answer Key

Monday
1. 8,771
2. 999
3. 300,068
4. 1, 2, 4, 5, 10, and 20
5. 45 cherries

Tuesday
1. 1,463
2. 423
3. even
4. 6 to 17 or 6:17
5. 11:10 A.M.

Wednesday
1. 12
2. 54
3. 0.5 or .5
4. 11
5. 8 years old

Thursday
1. 6   4. 1,000
2. 1   5. 4 engines
3. ☆ ▲ ☆

Friday
There are 13 different combinations. One possible organized list is:

Quarters	Dimes	Nickels	Pennies
1	0	0	2
0	1	0	17
0	1	1	12
0	1	2	7
0	1	3	2
0	2	0	7
0	2	1	2
0	0	1	22
0	0	2	17
0	0	3	12
0	0	4	7
0	0	5	2
0	0	0	27

Name: _____

1. 37.5
      + 42.1

2. 2,857 + 1,134 = _____

3. Order these lengths from shortest to longest.

  1 foot, 2 yards, 18 inches, 3 feet

  _____

4. Fill in the correct symbol.

  < = >

  79 ◯ 43

5. Don and Beth have birthdays that are 15 days apart. Don's birthday is on April 29th and Beth's birthday is after his. When is Beth's birthday?

  _____

Name: _____

1. 83.5
      − 61.2

2. 7,293 − 1,546 = _____

3. What is the range of this data?

  36, 75, 63, 49, 83, 46, 54, 79

  _____

4. Mark an **X** on this number line to show 13.

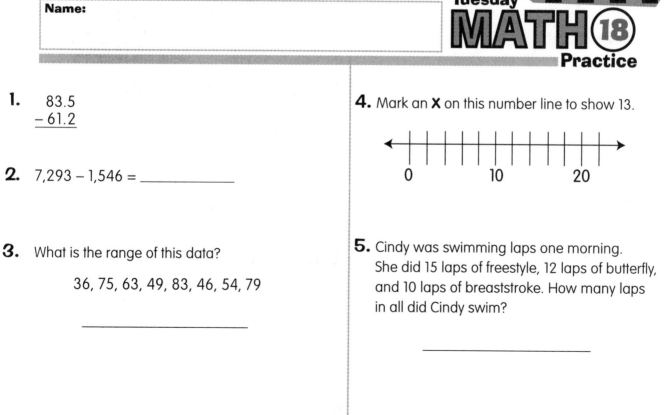

5. Cindy was swimming laps one morning. She did 15 laps of freestyle, 12 laps of butterfly, and 10 laps of breaststroke. How many laps in all did Cindy swim?

  _____

Name:

1.
$$\begin{array}{r} 6 \\ \times\ 6 \\ \hline \end{array}$$

2. $3 \times 10 =$ _____

3. How many cubes were used to make this figure?

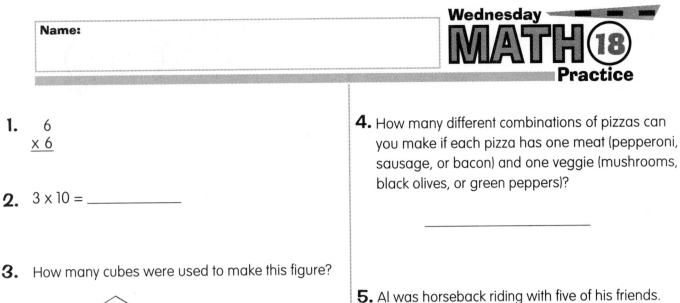

_____

4. How many different combinations of pizzas can you make if each pizza has one meat (pepperoni, sausage, or bacon) and one veggie (mushrooms, black olives, or green peppers)?

_____

5. Al was horseback riding with five of his friends. They rode for three hours and they each had to pay $5 per hour. How much did they have to pay altogether?

_____

Name:

1. $9\overline{)27}$

2. $16 \div 4 =$ _____

3. Estimate the sum of 62, 61, and 58.

_____

4. What fraction of this region is shaded?

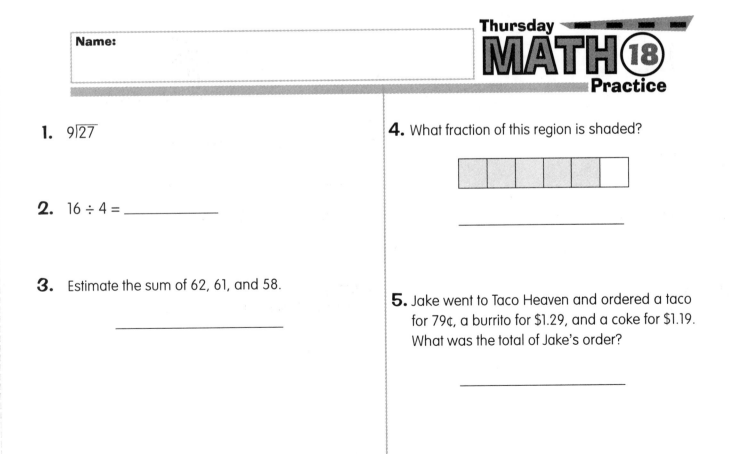

_____

5. Jake went to Taco Heaven and ordered a taco for 79¢, a burrito for $1.29, and a coke for $1.19. What was the total of Jake's order?

_____

Use the following clues to solve this problem. Notice that each section of the figure below is labeled with a letter. Your task is to find out what whole number goes in each region and what color it should be.

1. The sum of the triangle is 15.

2. The region that is in all three shapes is colored green.

3. The rectangle has the red, white, and green regions in it.

4. The orange region is the number 8.

5. The product of the D section and the blue section is 21.

6. The 5 region is purple.

7. A is red.

8. The sum of the rectangle is 11.

9. E is blue.

10. The sum of the circle is 20.

11. The sum of A and B is 8.

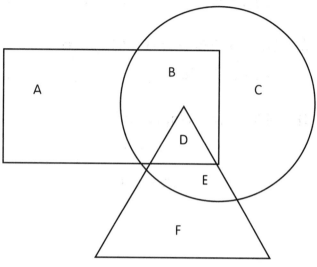

Answer Key

Monday

1. 79.6
2. 3,991
3. 1 foot, 18 inches, 3 feet, 2 yards
4. > (more than)
5. May 14th

Tuesday

1. 22.3
2. 5,747
3. 47
4. [number line marked between 10 and 20]
5. 37 laps

Wednesday

1. 36
2. 30
3. 15 cubes
4. 9 different pizzas
5. $90

Thursday

1. 3
2. 4
3. There are many possible answers, including 60 + 60 + 60 = 180.
4. $\frac{5}{6}$
5. $3.27

Friday

A–6–red, B–2–white, C–8–orange, D–3–green, E–7–blue, F–5–purple

Name:

1. Correct any mistakes or write "correct."

263.5 + 122.4 = 385.9 _____

2. Correct any mistakes or write "correct."

367 − 289 = 188 _____

3. Fill in the correct symbol.

< = >

29 ◯ 47

4. How many kilograms equal 3,000 grams?

_____

5. Judy is threading beads onto a string to make a necklace. She can fit 9 beads in one inch, and she wants the necklace to be 18 inches long. How many beads will she need?

_____

Name:

1. 11
      x 5

2. 32 ÷ 8 = _____

3. What is the perimeter of this figure?

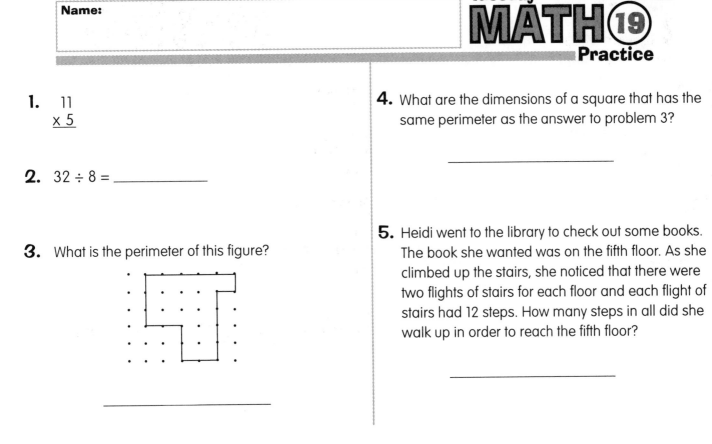

_____

4. What are the dimensions of a square that has the same perimeter as the answer to problem 3?

_____

5. Heidi went to the library to check out some books. The book she wanted was on the fifth floor. As she climbed up the stairs, she noticed that there were two flights of stairs for each floor and each flight of stairs had 12 steps. How many steps in all did she walk up in order to reach the fifth floor?

_____

Name:

1. Add one operational sign to make the equation true.

1 2 3 4 = 46

2. Add a sign.

4 6 8 = 38

3. What is the place value of the 3 in 93,764?

_____

4. List the first four multiples of 5.

_____

5. Martha was climbing up a rope that was attached to the gymnasium ceiling. The ceiling is 20 feet high, and she climbed to within 18 inches of the ceiling. How high did Martha climb?

_____

Name:

1. 5)‾2‾0‾

2. 111
    x 9

3. What are the next two numbers in this pattern?

100, 92, 84, 76, ____, ____

4. Which figure fits into the white space?

A   B   C   D

5. Laura was baby-sitting five kids for two hours. If she was paid $2 per kid per hour, how much money did Laura make that evening?

_____

Daily Math Practice, Grade 4 • EMC 753

Steve has listed his weekly math scores over the last nine weeks:

60, 72, 74, 80, 83, 85, 87, 92, 95

Make a graph to represent this data. Use a piece of graph paper or the space below.

Answer Key

MATH ⑲
Practice

Monday

1. correct
2. $367 - 289 = 78$
3. < (less than)
4. 3
5. 162 beads

Tuesday

1. 55
2. 4
3. 20 units
4. 5 units by 5 units
5. 96 steps

Wednesday

1. $12 + 34 = 46$
2. $46 - 8 = 38$
3. thousands
4. 5, 10, 15, and 20
5. $18\frac{1}{2}$ feet

Thursday

1. 4
2. 999
3. 68, 60
4. A
5. $20

Friday

A line graph or a bar graph are two possible choices.

Name: _____

1. Correct any mistakes or write "correct."

$3 \times 23 = 66$ _____

2. Correct any mistakes or write "correct."

$14.3 + 26.6 = 40.9$ _____

3. Write $\frac{1}{2}$ as a decimal.

_____

4. If the temperature outside is 54 degrees and it drops 18 degrees, what will the temperature be?

_____

5. Glenn is waiting for his ride after school. He got out of school at 3:20 and his mom is picking him up 25 minutes later. At what time will his mom pick him up?

_____

Name: _____

1.
$$\begin{array}{r} 100 \\ \times\ \ 8 \\ \hline \end{array}$$

2. $90 \div 9 =$ _____

3. If there are 6 red tiles and 5 blue tiles in a box, what are the chances that you will pick a red tile without looking?

_____

4. Write the number 285 in word form.

_____

5. Anita is watching a football game on TV. She has noticed that every 5 minutes there are 2 commercials. If the game lasts 2 hours, how many commercials will Anita see?

_____

Name: _____

1. Add a sign.

6 1 2 = 72

2. Add a sign.

9 8 1 2 = 86

3. Which figure is congruent to the first shape?

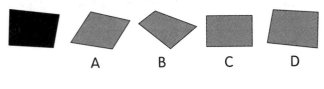

A   B   C   D

4. What is the tenth letter of the alphabet?

_____

5. Darian is playing in a piano recital. There are 12 kids each playing two songs in the recital. If each song takes an average of 3 minutes to play, how long will the recital last?

_____

Name: _____

1. 6⟌12

2. 101
      × 6
    ———

3. Round 389,935 to the nearest hundred thousand.

_____

4. Which is longer, 1 foot or 1 meter?

_____

5. Lucy has a library book that is 6 days overdue. The library charges 45¢ for the first day and 25¢ each additional day that a book is overdue. How much does Lucy owe the library in overdue fines?

_____

This figure is a sample of the concept of triangular numbers.
It shows 15 circles in the shape of a triangle.
The smallest triangular number is 3.
Draw four other examples of triangular numbers.

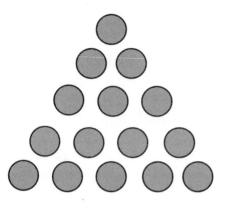

MATH 20
Practice

Answer Key

Monday

1. 3 x 23 = 69
2. correct
3. 0.5
4. 36 degrees
5. 3:45

Tuesday

1. 800
2. 10
3. 6 out of 11 or $\frac{6}{11}$
4. two hundred eighty-five
5. 48 commercials

Wednesday

1. 6 x 12 = 72
2. 98 – 12 = 86
3. D
4. J
5. 72 minutes or 1 hour and 12 minutes

Thursday

1. 2
2. 606
3. 400,000
4. 1 meter
5. $1.70

Friday

Answers will vary, including:

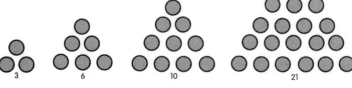

Name:

1. Correct any mistakes or write "correct."

$81 \div 9 = 9$ _____

2. Correct any mistakes or write "correct."

$155 - 138 = 117$ _____

3. Estimate the sum of 32, 29, 33, and 28.

_____

4. List all the factors of 16.

_____

5. Lynn was picking flowers to make a bouquet for her grandmother. She picked 5 roses, 6 daisies, and 7 daffodils. How many flowers were in the bouquet?

_____

Name:

1. $8\overline{)24}$

2. $\begin{array}{r} 43 \\ \times\ 2 \\ \hline \end{array}$

3. Which is larger, 0.3 or 0.8?

_____

4. What is the area of this rectangle?

_____

5. Alec has five shelves in his closet, each filled with toys. If there are 9 toys on each shelf, how many toys are there altogether?

_____

1. Add a sign.

9 6 8 = 12

2. Add a sign.

3 6 4 = 32

3. What are the coordinates of point **X** on this graph?

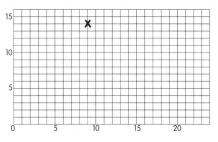

_____

4. If $Y = 4$, then what does $Y + Y$ equal?

_____

5. Lindy had 23 beanbags and gave 7 to her friend Shelley. How many does Lindy have left?

_____

1. $24 \div 3 =$ _____

2. 110
       x   7

3. Write 0.25 as a fraction.

_____

4. How many lines of symmetry does this figure have?

_____

5. Randy and Michelle were climbing trees and picking apples to help their mom make some pies. She said she wanted to make 9 pies and that she needed about 4 apples for each pie. How many apples do Randy and Michelle need to pick in order to have enough for the pies?

_____

These figures are all Nowats:

None of these are Nowats:

What makes something a Nowat? According to your definition, draw three other figures that are Nowats.

MATH 21
Practice

Answer Key

Monday
1. correct
2. 155 – 138 = 17
3. 120 (30 × 4)
4. 1, 2, 4, 8, and 16
5. 18 flowers

Tuesday
1. 3
2. 86
3. 0.8
4. 12 square units
5. 45 toys

Wednesday
1. 96 ÷ 8 = 12
2. 36 – 4 = 32
3. (9, 14)
4. 8
5. 16 beanbags

Thursday
1. 8
2. 770
3. $\frac{1}{4}$
4. 2
5. 36 apples

Friday
Nowats are figures that have a straight line drawn horizontally across them. Students' drawings will vary, but may include figures such as:

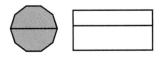

1. Correct any mistakes or write "correct."

$4 \times 24 = 88$ _____

2. Correct any mistakes or write "correct."

$18 \div 6 = 3$ _____

3. Is 294 odd or even?

_____

4. What is the inverse of division?

_____

5. As Dean was finishing his homework last night, he realized that he had done 8 pages of math. If there were 60 problems in all, how many problems were on each page?

_____

1. $4\overline{)40}$

2. $\begin{array}{r} \frac{7}{8} \\ - \frac{5}{8} \\ \hline \end{array}$

3. Which is larger, $\frac{1}{2}$ or $\frac{1}{4}$?

_____

4. Using this function machine, if you input 8, the output would be 18. What would the output be if the input is 12?

_____

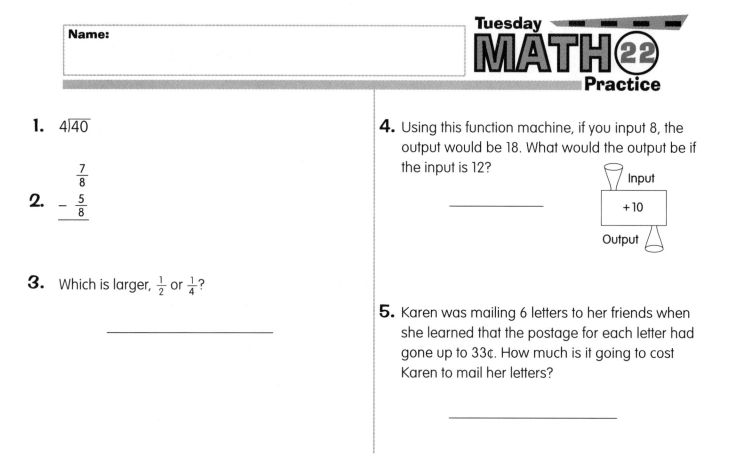

Input

+10

Output

5. Karen was mailing 6 letters to her friends when she learned that the postage for each letter had gone up to 33¢. How much is it going to cost Karen to mail her letters?

_____

1. Add a sign.

3 5 1 1 = 46

2. Add a sign.

7 1 0 = 70

3. I am a number between 10 and 25. I am a multiple of 8, and one of my digits is a 2. What number am I?

_____

4. When this is folded into a cube, which letter is on the side opposite the D?

_____

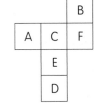

5. Pamela is collecting stickers from different states in the United States. She has some from 34 states. If she wants to get stickers from every state, how many more does she need to get?

_____

---

1.   105
    x   9

2. 36 ÷ 9 = _____

3. How many cups are in 3 quarts?

_____

4. What is the median (or middle value) of this data?

44, 48, 52, 54, 58, 63, 65

_____

5. When Carmen got up this morning it was 42 degrees outside. By 2:00 in the afternoon the temperature had risen 39 degrees. What was the temperature at 2:00?

_____

Austin has a coupon for 50% off at King Grocery. He can buy a video there whose original price is $14.98. Another store, Safemart, has the same video on sale for $7.99.

Which store has the better buy? Why?

_____

_____

_____

Answer Key

MATH ②②
Practice

Monday

1. 4 x 24 = 96
2. correct
3. even
4. multiplication
5. 7 to 8 problems per page

Tuesday

1. 10
2. $\frac{2}{8}$
3. $\frac{1}{2}$
4. 22
5. $1.98

Wednesday

1. 35 + 11 = 46
2. 7 x 10 = 70
3. 24
4. C
5. 16 more stickers

Thursday

1. 945
2. 4
3. 12 cups
4. 54
5. 81 degrees

Friday

King Grocery has the better buy because if you take 50% off, the video will cost only $7.49, while Safemart has it for $7.99, 50¢ more than King Grocery.

Name:

1. Correct any mistakes or write "correct."

5 x 40 = 200 _____

2. Correct any mistakes or write "correct."

157.4 − 92.9 = 64.5 _____

3. What place value does the 8 have in 15.8?

_____

4. Fill in the correct symbol.

< = >

73 ◯ 7.4

5. Fred is collecting shells on the beach. If he finds a shell every three steps that he takes, how many shells will he find after taking 30 steps?

_____

Name:

1. 10 ÷ 5 = _____

2. 141
x 7

3. What are the next two numbers in this pattern?

6, 13, 27, 55, _____, _____

4. How many rectangles are in this figure?

_____

5. Isabelle is going across the monkey bars at school. There are 16 bars on the monkey bars. If she starts with the first bar and skips two bars each time she swings, how many bars will Isabelle touch in all?

_____

1. Add a sign.

1 2 3 8 = 131

2. Add a sign.

1 5 4 1 2 = 142

3. How much are 15 dimes worth?

_____

4. Mark an **X** on the number line to show 13.

5. Seth was digging up weeds in his backyard. His dad agreed to pay him 5¢ for each weed he pulls. If he pulls 208 weeds, how much will his dad pay him?

_____

1. $10\overline{)20}$

2.
$$\begin{array}{r} 106 \\ \times\ \ 8 \\ \hline \end{array}$$

3. How do you know if a number is divisible by 5?

_____

_____

4. A soup recipe calls for $1\frac{1}{4}$ pounds of pinto beans. The package of beans is labeled 28 ounces. Is that enough?

_____

5. Shirley is going to the store to buy a can of soup for her mom. A 3-ounce can of soup costs 33¢ and a 12-ounce can of soup costs $1.20. Which one is the better buy?

_____

This cube contains 8 cubes. The four sides of each cube are shaded light gray and dark gray (opposite sides are shaded the same). The top and bottom alternate white and black.

Sketch and shade what you think the cube would look like if you were looking at it from where the arrow is pointing.

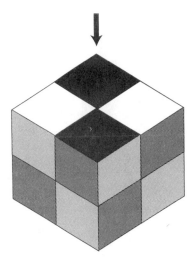

Answer Key

MATH 23
Practice

Monday
1. correct
2. correct
3. tenths
4. > (more than)
5. 10 shells

Tuesday
1. 2
2. 987
3. 111, 223
4. 16 rectangles
5. 6 bars

Wednesday
1. 123 + 8 = 131
2. 154 − 12 = 142
3. $1.50
4.
5. $10.40

Thursday
1. 2
2. 848
3. A number is divisible by 5 if the digit in the ones place is a 5 or a 0.
4. Yes—$1\frac{1}{4}$ pounds = 20 ounces
5. The 12-ounce can for $1.20 is the better buy, because if you bought 4 of the other cans (3 oz.) they would cost $1.32.

Friday
It is exactly the same when you look at this cube from the other side.

1. Correct any mistakes or write "correct."

79.3 + 12.7 = 82.1 _____

2. Correct any mistakes or write "correct."

900 ÷ 9 = 100 _____

3. Which cube comes next in this pattern?

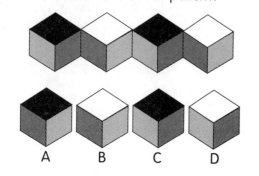

   A   B   C   D

4. Order these numbers from smallest to largest.

0.9 $\frac{3}{4}$ 0.5 $\frac{1}{3}$ $1\frac{1}{4}$

_____

5. Bruce is a very fast reader and reads about 40 pages in an hour. If he has a 140-page book, about how long will it take him to read it?

_____

1. 3 x 327 = _____

2. 6)‾66‾

3. Construct a graph to represent this information. Use a piece of graph paper or the back of this page.

Favorite Musical	Boys	Girls
Sound of Music	2	5
West Side Story	8	3
Oklahoma	4	3
Singing in the Rain	3	4

4. Write the number six hundred two in standard notation.

_____

5. Julia just finished a spelling test and thinks that she got most of the words right. She guessed on 10 out of the 100 words. If she gets half of those that she guessed on right and all of the other ones right, how many words will she get wrong on the whole test?

_____

1. Add a sign.

1 0 0 1 0 = 10

2. Add a sign.

1 2 8 = 28

3. List the first three multiples of 9.

_____

4. How many edges does a cube have?

_____

5. Allen and Geoff are mowing lawns together to raise money to go to summer camp. One day last week, they were paid $10 for one lawn, $16 for another, and $18 for yet another. They put all the money together and then split it in half. How much did each boy earn that day?

_____

1. 300 ÷ 10 = _____

2. 1,041
   x   6

3. How many feet are in 3 yards?

_____

4. What is the perimeter of this rectangle?

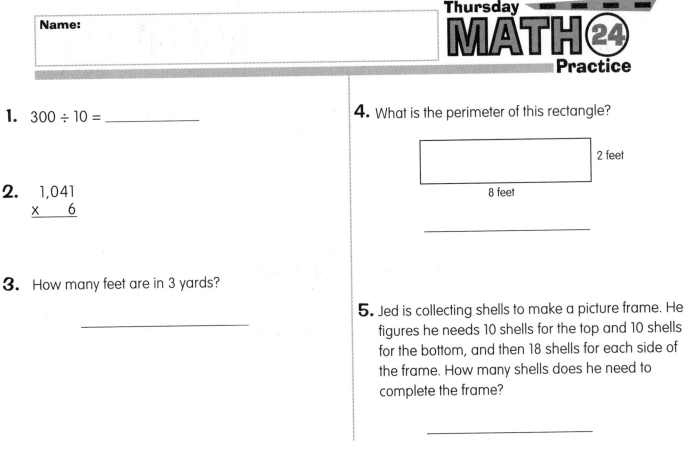

2 feet

8 feet

_____

5. Jed is collecting shells to make a picture frame. He figures he needs 10 shells for the top and 10 shells for the bottom, and then 18 shells for each side of the frame. How many shells does he need to complete the frame?

_____

Daily Math Practice, Grade 4 • EMC 753

This clock represents the time that a birthday party ended. Bobby opened his presents 45 minutes before this time. The kids were all eating cake 25 minutes before that. They were all playing games 30 minutes before that. The party actually started 20 minutes before that.

At what time did the birthday party start?

_____

Answer Key

Monday
1. 79.3 + 12.7 = 92.0
2. correct
3. C
4. $\frac{1}{3}$, 0.5, $\frac{3}{4}$, 0.9, $1\frac{1}{4}$
5. about $3\frac{1}{2}$ hours

Tuesday
1. 981
2. 11
3. One possible graph:

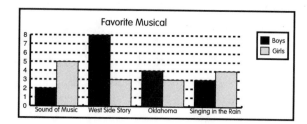

4. 602
5. 5 words

Wednesday
1. 100 ÷ 10 = 10
2. 1 x 28 = 28
3. 9, 18, 27
4. 12
5. Each boy earned $22.

Thursday
1. 30
2. 6,246
3. 9 feet
4. 20 feet
5. 56 shells

Friday
The birthday party started at 12:30.

1. Correct any mistakes or write "correct."

2 x 345 = 708 _____

2. Correct any mistakes or write "correct."

206.4 – 103.8 = 102.6 _____

3. Dianna and Becky were playing on the same soccer team and took turns being goalie. They stopped 9 out of every 10 shots made against them. If the other team scored 3 points, how many balls did Dianna and Becky stop from going into the net?

_____

4. Using this graph, how many students in all have brown eyes?

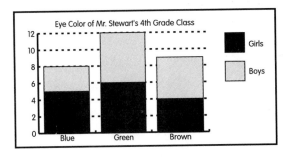

Eye Color of Mr. Stewart's 4th Grade Class

Girls
Boys
Blue   Green   Brown

_____

5. Using the graph in problem 4, how many boys have blue eyes?

_____

1. 21 ÷ 7 = _____

2. 2,162
   x   4

3. Round 998 to the nearest thousand.

_____

4. If $m = 6$, then what does $m - 3$ equal?

_____

5. Dale and Kendra were sweeping out their garage when they found 6 boxes each filled with hats. If there were about 15 hats in each box, how many hats were there altogether?

_____

1. Add a sign.

   1 5 6 8 = 164

2. Add a sign.

   9 0 5 = 18

3. How many blocks are in this figure?

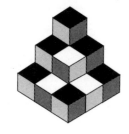

_____

4. Which is smaller, 0.30 or 0.08?

_____

5. Kyle and Brad were playing video games for 3 hours and 45 minutes last Friday night. If they started at 5:50 P.M. and played straight through, at what time did they stop playing the video games?

_____

1. 8)‾5‾6‾8‾

2.   1,041
       x   8

3. List all the factors of 20.

_____

4. Which figure is congruent to the first figure?

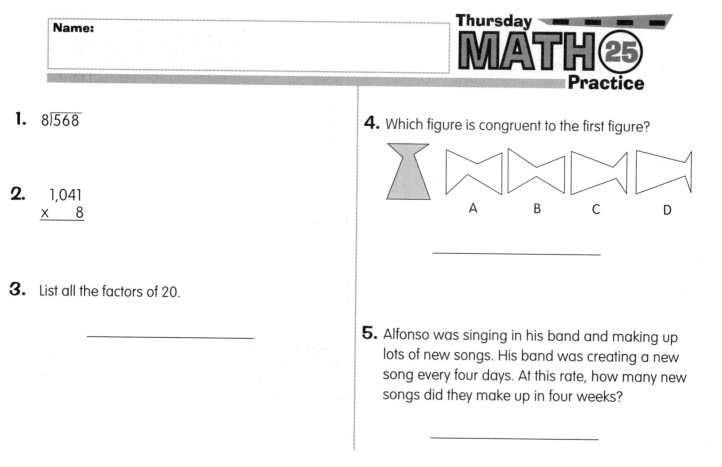

_____

5. Alfonso was singing in his band and making up lots of new songs. His band was creating a new song every four days. At this rate, how many new songs did they make up in four weeks?

_____

Harry has $6.28 in his pocket. What is the largest number of quarters he could have?

_____

What is the largest number of dimes he could have?

_____

Why do you think these are the correct answers?

_____

_____

_____

Answer Key

Monday
1. 2 x 345 = 690
2. correct
3. 27 balls
4. There are 9 students that have brown eyes.
5. There are 3 boys that have blue eyes.

Tuesday
1. 3
2. 8,648
3. 1,000
4. 3
5. about 90 hats

Wednesday
1. 156 + 8 = 164
2. 90 ÷ 5 = 18
3. 14 blocks
4. 0.08
5. 9:35 P.M.

Thursday
1. 71
2. 8,328
3. 1, 2, 4, 5, 10, and 20
4. C
5. 7 new songs

Friday
The largest number of quarters he could have is 25, because that alone would equal $6.25, leaving only 3¢ to be in pennies. The largest number of dimes he could have is 62, because that would total $6.20, leaving only 8¢, not enough to make another dime.

Daily Math Practice, Grade 4 • EMC 753

1. Correct any mistakes or write "correct."

   648 ÷ 8 = 71 _____

2. Correct any mistakes or write "correct."

   47.4 − 29.5 = 17.9 _____

3. Estimate 11 × 299.

   _____

4. Which fraction is larger, $\frac{1}{4}$ or $\frac{2}{3}$?

   _____

5. Thomas and Tate were walking to school when they saw their friends walking in front of them. They decided to run and catch up with them. When they joined up with their friends, their hearts were beating about 24 beats every ten seconds. At this rate, about how many times would one of their hearts beat in 3 minutes?

   _____

1. $2\overline{)268}$

2. $\begin{array}{r} \frac{3}{4} \\ -\frac{2}{8} \\ \hline \end{array}$

3. Draw the rest of this figure if the line drawn is a line of symmetry.

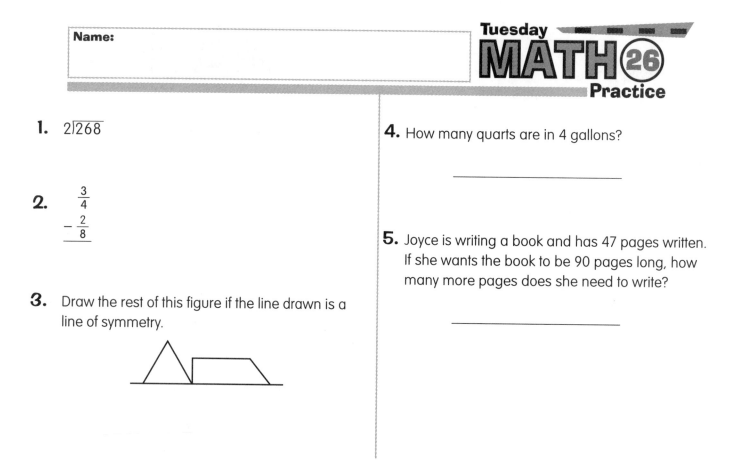

4. How many quarts are in 4 gallons?

   _____

5. Joyce is writing a book and has 47 pages written. If she wants the book to be 90 pages long, how many more pages does she need to write?

   _____

1. Add a sign.

5 1 2 = 60

2. Add a sign.

2 0 8 = 160

3. What temperature is 16 degrees below 45 degrees?

_____

4. What is the area of this shape?

_____

5. Mindy was born in 1988. If Mindy's brother is exactly 3 years younger than her, in what year was he born?

_____

1. 1,510
    x   5

2. $54 \div 9 =$ _____

3. What is the probability of getting two heads when two coins are flipped?

_____

4. Label the angles: right, acute, obtuse.

_____ _____ _____

5. If Leo, Jessie, and Franchesca are going to a movie, in how many different ways can they line up to buy their tickets?

_____

Use the digits 1 through 9 to complete these number sentences. Use each digit only once.
Are there any other possible solutions?

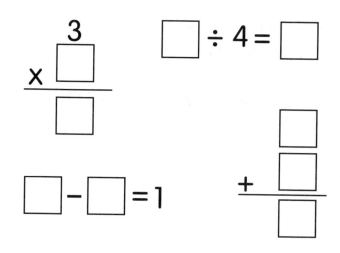

Answer Key

Monday
1. $648 \div 8 = 81$
2. correct
3. 3,000 (10 x 300)
4. $\frac{2}{3}$
5. about 432 beats in 3 minutes

Tuesday
1. 134
2. $\frac{4}{8}$ or $\frac{1}{2}$
3.
4. 16 quarts
5. 43 more pages

Wednesday
1. $5 \times 12 = 60$
2. $20 \times 8 = 160$
3. 29 degrees
4. 23 square units
5. 1991

Thursday
1. 7,550
2. 6
3. 1 out of 4 or $\frac{1}{4}$
4. obtuse, right, acute
5. 6 different ways

Friday
There are many possible solutions. One solution is:

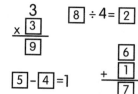

Daily Math Practice, Grade 4 • EMC 753

1. Correct any mistakes or write "correct."

$30 \div 5 = 6$ _____

2. Correct any mistakes or write "correct."

$14 + 35 + 10 = 59$ _____

3. Mark an **X** on the graph where point (13, 8) would be located.

4. What are the next three numbers in this pattern?

80, 70, 60, _____, _____, _____

5. Justin and Tanna were racing across the school yard. Tanna made it in 1 minute and 18 seconds, while Justin ran it in 75 seconds. Who was faster? Why?

_____

_____

_____

_____

1. $6\overline{)606}$

2.
$$\begin{array}{r} 104 \\ \times \ 9 \\ \hline \end{array}$$

3. What number can you add to any number you want and always get that same number as the answer?

_____

4. What is the mode (most frequently appearing item) of this data?

36, 38, 40, 40, 42, 45, 45, 45, 48, 57

_____

5. Norma and Kris were throwing rocks into the river as they walked along the shore. Every three steps, they would each throw 1 stone. If they each walked 90 steps, how many rocks were thrown into the river by both Norma and Kris?

_____

1. Add a sign.

1 0 5 5 = 21

2. Add a sign.

8 9 8 = 81

3. What flat shape has four sides that are all the same length, but no right angles?

_____

4. Here are three different views of a cube. What number is on the side opposite the 5?

_____

5. Mike is walking his younger brother to school. If Mike is 12 and twice as old as his brother, how old is his brother?

_____

1. 427 ÷ 7 = _____

2.   1,051
       x   7

3. What place value does the 8 have in 80,497?

_____

4. Victor drew an equilateral triangle. He made the base 4 centimeters long. How long were each of the other two sides?

_____

5. Cheryl is washing her dogs in the driveway. She fills a tub with 20 gallons of water to begin with. Then she uses another 28 gallons of water to rinse the dogs. Finally, she uses 9 gallons of water to clean the driveway. How much water did Cheryl use?

_____

If you put a 6 into this first machine, 24 comes out. Write three different rules that could be taking place.

6
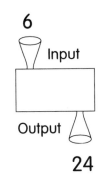
Input

Output

24

_____

_____

_____

After you have your three rules, test to see if any of them work if you put 8 into the machine and get 28. If not, can you figure out one rule that works for BOTH of these pairs of numbers?

8
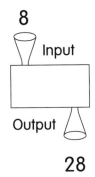
Input

Output

28

_____

_____

_____

MATH ⓗ
Practice

Answer Key

Monday

1. correct
2. correct
3.

4. 50, 40, 30
5. Justin was faster, because Tanna took 78 seconds, while Justin took only 75 seconds.

Tuesday

1. 101
2. 936
3. 0
4. 45
5. 60 stones (30 stones each)

Wednesday

1. $105 \div 5 = 21$
2. $89 - 8 = 81$
3. parallelogram
4. 2
5. 6 years old

Thursday

1. 61
2. 7,357
3. ten-thousands
4. 4 centimeters
5. 57 gallons

Friday

There are many possible answers for the first one, including: Multiply the input by 4 OR add 18 to the input. The rule that works for BOTH is double the input and add 12.

1. Correct any mistakes or write "correct."

$9,053 - 6,845 = 3,208$ _____

2. Correct any mistakes or write "correct."

$201.6 + 725.4 = 927.0$ _____

3. Write the number three thousand sixty-eight in standard form.

_____

4. List the first four multiples of 2.

_____

5. Toby has a watch that runs at half the speed it should. In other words, the hands on his watch move a half-hour when an hour of time has really passed. Toby's watch is correct at 8:00 A.M. What time will Toby's watch say when the real time is 10:30 A.M.?

_____

---

1. $763 \div 7 =$ _____

2. $\begin{array}{r} 256 \\ \times\ \ 2 \\ \hline \end{array}$

3. What are the next two figures in this pattern?

♣ ♥ ♥ ♣ ♦ ♣ ♥ ♥ ♣ ♦ _____ _____

4. What three-dimensional shape is a basketball?

_____

5. Jeremy wants to go whale watching with his friends while they are on vacation in California. There are six kids who want to go, and it will cost each one $38. How much will it cost for all six?

_____

Name:

1. Add a sign.

8 1 2 = 20

2. Add a sign.

5 9 1 2 = 71

3. Amber was roller blading down her street. Ten minutes after starting, she crashed into her friend's bike. If she started roller blading at 4:55 P.M., at what time did she crash into the bike?

_____

4. This graph shows how Marissa spent the $40 that she earned from baby-sitting. Approximately how much money did she spend on food?

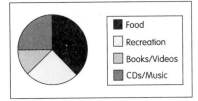

■ Food
□ Recreation
▨ Books/Videos
▦ CDs/Music

_____

5. Which weighs more, 1 gram or 1 pound?

_____

Name:

1. 3⟌2,136

2.   136
      x   5

3. What is the perimeter of this diagram?

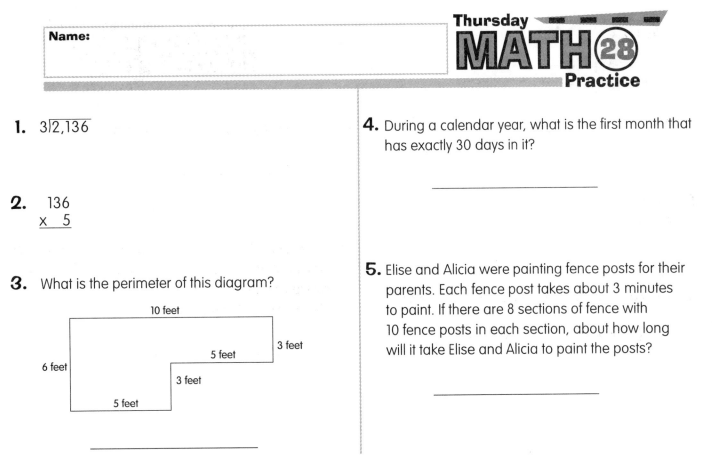

10 feet
3 feet
5 feet
6 feet
3 feet
5 feet

_____

4. During a calendar year, what is the first month that has exactly 30 days in it?

_____

5. Elise and Alicia were painting fence posts for their parents. Each fence post takes about 3 minutes to paint. If there are 8 sections of fence with 10 fence posts in each section, about how long will it take Elise and Alicia to paint the posts?

_____

Use the following clues to determine the order of the six bus stops. The bus stops at the closest house first, then the second, and so forth until it gets to the house that is farthest from the school.

1. Ginger lives farther from school than Henry, but not as far as Lou.

2. Henry lives closer to the school than Dan.

3. Karla lives closer to the school than Vicki.

4. Karla lives closer to the school than Dan, but farther than Ginger.

5. Vicki is the last stop.

6. Lou's stop is immediately after Karla's.

MATH 28
Practice

Answer Key

Monday
1. 9,053 − 6,845 = 2,208
2. correct
3. 3,068
4. 2, 4, 6, and 8
5. 9:15 A.M.

Tuesday
1. 109
2. 512
3. ♣ ♥
4. sphere
5. $228

Wednesday
1. 8 + 12 = 20
2. 59 + 12 = 71
3. 5:05 P.M.
4. about $15; accept anything in the range of $12 to $18
5. 1 pound

Thursday
1. 712
2. 680
3. 32 feet
4. April
5. about 240 minutes or 4 hours

Friday
After leaving the school, the bus stops at Henry's, Ginger's, Karla's, Lou's, Dan's, and then Vicki's.

Name:

1. Correct any mistakes or write "correct."

$3 \times 298 = 874$ _____

2. Correct any mistakes or write "correct."

$17.5 - 16.8 = 0.7$ _____

3. Round 39,274 to the nearest thousand.

_____

4. Draw the radius of circle 1. Draw the diameter of circle 2.

circle 1   circle 2

5. Marcus is playing dodge ball with some of his friends during recess. He catches 2 out of every 5 balls that are thrown in his direction. If he catches 14 balls, how many were thrown toward him?

_____

Name:

1. $4,806 \div 6 =$ _____

2. $\begin{array}{r} 1,507 \\ \times \quad 6 \\ \hline \end{array}$

3. List all the factors of 6 and 8.

_____

4. Using the factors you listed in problem 3, what factors are common to both?

_____

5. Emi is baby-sitting for $4.00 per hour, and the couple plans to be gone for 6 hours. Emi's friend wants to come over and help out, so they will share the money. If they split the money evenly, how much will Emi get?

_____

1. Add a sign.

4 9 6 9 2 = 404

2. Add a sign.

1 5 3 = 45

3. If the dark line represents a line of symmetry, draw the rest of the figure.

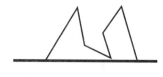

4. How many inches are in 4 feet?

_____

5. Stan is delivering papers to save money for a new stereo. He makes 4¢ for each paper he delivers each day. If he delivers 40 papers each day, how much does he make in a month (30 days)?

_____

---

1. $10\overline{)700}$

2.
```
  1,118
x     8
```

3. Yasmin was building new shelves for her books. She figured she could fit about 30 books on each shelf. If she has about 200 books, how many shelves does she need?

_____

4. If $r = 10$, then what is $r + 15$?

_____

5. Looking at this graph, what question do you think was asked in the survey? How many more voted for Math than for Reading?

10
8
6
4
2
0

Math Reading Science Writing Social Studies

_____

_____

Name:

Use the digits 3, 6, 8, and 9 to answer these questions. Use each digit only once for each question.

1. What is the smallest even number you can make? _____

2. What is the largest number you can make? _____

3. List all the 4-digit numbers you can make that are multiples of 5.

_____

4. List all the 4-digit numbers you can make that are multiples of 4.

_____

Answer Key

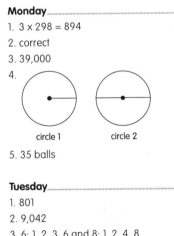

1. Correct any mistakes or write "correct."

$3,228 \div 4 = 807$ _____

2. Correct any mistakes or write "correct."

$12 + 63 + 8 = 73$ _____

3. Which holds more, 1 gallon or 1 liter?

_____

4. How many dimes are in a roll that is worth $2.00?

_____

5. Janet was washing the glasses and putting them away in the cupboard. She noticed that she could stack a maximum of 4 glasses on top of each other. If she has 23 glasses to put away, what is the minimum number of stacks she will need to make?

_____

1. $5\overline{)255}$

2. $\begin{array}{r} 10 \\ \times 25 \\ \hline \end{array}$

3. Estimate the difference of $198 - 49$.

_____

4. Fill in the correct symbol.

$< = >$

$17 \bigcirc 2.95$

5. Gary is building a doghouse. He needs to buy nails and is counting the number he needs for each side. The roof needs 20 nails, the front and back each need 15 nails, and the two sides need 12 nails each. The bottom needs another 18 nails. How many nails altogether does Gary need to buy?

_____

1. Add a sign.

1 0 2 = 5

2. Add a sign.

4 2 7 = 6

3. Each section on the number line is one unit. Label each mark.

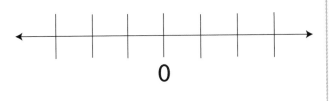

0

4. Which of these figures is congruent to the gray figure?

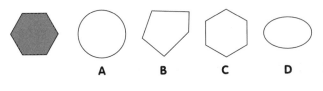

A   B   C   D

5. Leon was washing his parents' cars. His dad said he would pay him $4 to wash his car and another $4 to wash his mother's car. Then his older brother said that he would pay him $5 to wash his car. If Leon washes all three cars, how much money will he make?

_____

1. 3,024 ÷ 3 = _____

2.   12
   x 43

3. Mark an **X** on this number line to show 68.

25   50   75

4. How many cubes are in this rectangular prism?

_____

5. Tina was walking to school and noticed that 1 out of every 3 houses she passed had a dog in the backyard. If she passed 18 houses, how many dogs did she see?

_____

Nancy, Mark, and Ray are raising money for the homeless shelter in their town by having a walkathon. They are asking people to pledge a certain amount of money for each mile that they walk. Nancy has $3.20 pledged per mile, Mark has $5.15 pledged per mile, and Ray has $2.50 pledged per mile. If all three each walk 12 miles, what is the total amount of money they will raise for the homeless shelter?

_____

Answer Key

Monday
1. correct
2. 12 + 63 + 8 = 83
3. 1 gallon
4. 20
5. 6 stacks

Tuesday
1. 51
2. 250
3. There are many possible answers, including 150 (200 − 50).
4. > (more than)
5. 92 nails

Wednesday
1. 10 ÷ 2 = 5
2. 42 ÷ 7 = 6
3.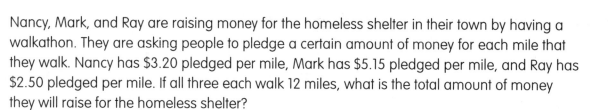
4. C
5. $13

Thursday
1. 1,008
2. 516
3.
4. 20 cubes
5. 6 dogs

Friday
$130.20

1. Correct any mistakes or write "correct."

823.6 + 147.5 = 970.1 _____

2. Correct any mistakes or write "correct."

954 − 396 = 558 _____

3. What place value does the 8 have in 10,978?

_____

4. Which is smaller, $\frac{1}{3}$ or $\frac{3}{4}$?

_____

5. Lian and Thelma are baking cookies for their Friday night party. There are going to be 12 people in addition to Lian and Thelma at the party, and they want to have enough cookies for each person to have three. How many cookies do they need to bake?

_____

---

1. 231
      x 13

2. 164 ÷ 4 = _____

3. If it was 8 degrees in the morning and the temperature dropped 10 degrees, what temperature is it now?

_____

4. What is the area of this figure?

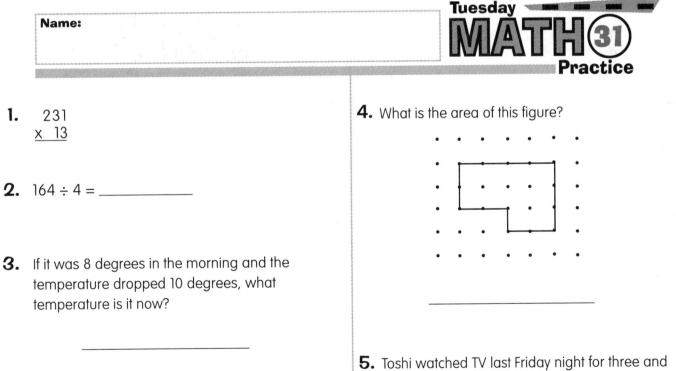

_____

5. Toshi watched TV last Friday night for three and one-half hours straight. If he started at 8:45 P.M., at what time did he finish watching TV?

_____

1. Add a sign.

2 1 0 = 0

2. Add a sign.

1 6 8 2 1 = 189

3. Construct a graph to represent this information. Use a piece of graph paper or the back of this page.

Pizza Toppings	Number of People
pepperoni	25
sausage	19
mushrooms	22
black olives	15
anchovies	3

4. What is the 6th letter of the alphabet?

_____

5. Derek and Joel were playing catch with a water balloon. They started out right next to each other. Every time they threw and successfully caught the balloon, they each had to step backwards 1 foot. They continued doing this until one of them missed the balloon, which happened after their 12th successful throw. How far apart were they at this time?

_____

---

1. $9\overline{)4,509}$

2. $\dfrac{12}{16}$
$-\dfrac{1}{4}$

3. What is the range of this data?

36, 38, 40, 40, 42, 45, 45, 45, 48, 57

_____

4. What is the probability that a white sock would be pulled from a drawer that has all white socks in it?

_____

5. Annie was picking dandelions in her backyard for her mother. Annie is only half as old as her sister Jane, who is half as old as their brother Evan. If Evan is 12, how old is Annie?

_____

This cube contains 27 cubes. The 4 sides of each cube alternate light gray and dark gray. The tops and bottoms alternate white and black. Sketch and shade what you think the cube in the very center looks like.

Why do you think the shading would look like that?

_____

_____

_____

_____

MATH 31
Practice

Answer Key

Monday
1. 823.6 + 147.5 = 971.1
2. correct
3. ones
4. $\frac{1}{3}$
5. 42 cookies

Tuesday
1. 3,003
2. 41
3. ‑2 degrees
4. 10 square units
5. 12:15 A.M.

Wednesday
1. 21 × 0 = 0
2. 168 + 21 = 189
3. There are many possible answers, including:
4. F
5. 24 feet

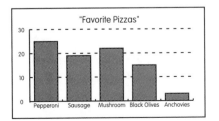

Thursday
1. 501
2. $\frac{8}{16}$ or $\frac{1}{2}$
3. 21
4. 1
5. 3 years old

Friday

Since each block alternates, we know that the top surface will be white because the top of the cube above it is black. Then, looking at the cubes with white on top, the darker shading is on the left.

Name:

1. Correct any mistakes or write "correct."

11 x 456 = 4,916 _____

2. Correct any mistakes or write "correct."

69.45 − 22.83 = 47.52 _____

3. Write the number 2,900 in word form.

_____

4. What number can you multiply times any number you pick and always get that same number as the answer?

_____

5. Zachary put a clicker on his bicycle wheel spoke, so every time it hits the top it clicks. If each click means that Zachary has gone one and one-half meters, how far has he gone after hearing 12 clicks?

_____

Name:

1.   101
     x 15

2. 4,024 ÷ 8 = _____

3. Sharise was coloring in her coloring book with her new box of 64 crayons. There were so many spaces in a particular design that she had to use each crayon 3 times. How many spaces were in that design?

_____

4. What could this graph be a representation of?

_____

_____

_____

5. What number would you predict as the next piece of data for the graph in problem 4?

_____

Name:

1. Add a sign.

8 2 2 = 41

2. Add a sign.

2 1 4 0 = 840

3. List the first four multiples of 3 and 4.

_____

4. Using the information you created in problem 3, what is the smallest multiple that is common to BOTH 3 and 4 (listed as a multiple of both numbers)?

_____

5. Juanita has four coins that total 50¢. What are the four coins?

_____

Name:

1. 9⟌729

2. 16
x 62

3. What are the next two numbers in this pattern?

5, 13, 29, 61, _____, _____

4. What shape has four sides and one pair of opposite sides that are parallel?

_____

5. Casey is thinking of a number. Use these clues to guess his number:

1. It is a three-digit number.
2. The ones digit is either 8 or 9.
3. The tens digit is 2 less than the ones digit.
4. The hundreds digit is 3 less than the tens digit.
5. The number is odd.

_____

Peter collects bugs and keeps them in a cage. Once a week he opens the lid to add some new bugs, but each time he does, 3 bugs get away. He adds 5 bugs at a time. If he starts with 18 bugs, how many bugs will he have at the end of 6 weeks?

_____

Draw a line graph representing this information. Use a piece of graph paper or the space below.

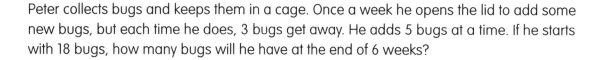

Answer Key

MATH 32
Practice

Monday

1. 11 x 456 = 5,016
2. 69.45 – 22.83 = 46.62
3. two thousand nine hundred
4. 1
5. 18 meters

Tuesday

1. 1,515
2. 503
3. 192 spaces
4. There are many possible answers, including: "High Temperatures for April" or "Number of Hot Lunches Eaten During March."
5. Since it seems to be increasing, students should be guessing a value somewhere in the range of 85 to 95.

Wednesday

1. 82 ÷ 2 = 41
2. 21 x 40 = 840
3. 3: 3, 6, 9, 12 and 4: 4, 8, 12, 16
4. 12
5. 1 quarter, 2 dimes, and 1 nickel

Thursday

1. 81
2. 992
3. 125 and 253 (double the previous one and add 3)
4. trapezoid
5. 479

Friday

At the end of the 6 weeks, he will have 30 bugs. There are many possible graphs, for example:

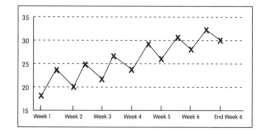

Name:

1. Correct any mistakes or write "correct."

$350 \div 5 = 70$ _____

2. Correct any mistakes or write "correct."

$45.3 + 17.3 = 52.6$ _____

3. Round 297,490 to the nearest ten-thousand.

_____

4. What would you get if you add 10 tenths together?

_____

5. Nolan plays baseball and loves to pitch. He throws a fantastic curve ball that only one-third of the batters can hit. If 45 players attempt to hit his curve ball, about how many actually hit it?

_____

Name:

1. $2\overline{)8,410}$

2. $\begin{array}{r} 27 \\ \times 76 \\ \hline \end{array}$

3. What are the next three figures in this pattern?

▲☆▲☆☆▲☆☆☆ ___ ___ ___

4. What is the ordered pair for point **X** on this graph?

_____

5. Erika has 5 more pencils than her friend Jana. If Jana has 13 pencils, how many does Erika have?

_____

1. Add a sign.

8 0 2 9 = 793

2. Add a sign.

2 5 2 1 = 4

3. Using this function machine, what would the output be if you put in 6?

Input

times 2
plus 1

Output

_____

4. Using the function machine in problem 3, what would your input be if your output was 9?

_____

5. Suzanne wants to buy a new ring that costs $27.00. She has $13.00 in her wallet and will get her $12.00 allowance tomorrow. How much more money does she need?

_____

1. 159 ÷ 3 = _____

2. 38
    x 57

3. What shape is the base of a cylinder?

_____

4. Mark any statement that is true about this angle.

○ It is an obtuse angle.

○ It is an acute angle.

○ The angle measures less than 90°.

○ The angle measures more than 90°.

5. Skip was counting his change and found that it totaled $6.73. He had 18 pennies, 14 quarters, 2 half-dollars, and 5 dimes. How many nickels did he have?

_____

Daily Math Practice, Grade 4 • EMC 753

Max, Angela, Veronica, and Mitch were all getting ready to go on their family vacations, all leaving from San Diego, California. Use the following clues to help you figure out the last name of each child, the child's vacation destination, and the mode of transportation used.

1. The Medina family went to Hawaii by either plane or ship.

2. Angela's family went by car to Wyoming.

3. Max's family went by train.

4. The Tseu family went to Florida.

5. The Carlson family did not go to New York, but another family did.

6. The Rodriguez boy got sick on the train ride he took on his vacation.

7. The Tseu's daughter is an only child.

8. The family going by airplane went to Florida for their vacation.

MATH 33
Practice

Answer Key

Monday
1. correct
2. 45.3 + 17.3 = 62.6
3. 300,000
4. 1 whole
5. 15 players

Tuesday
1. 4,205
2. 2,052
3. ▲ ☆ ☆
4. (22, 9)
5. 18 pencils

Wednesday
1. 802 − 9 = 793
2. 25 − 21 = 4
3. 13
4. 4
5. $2

Thursday
1. 53
2. 2,166
3. circle
4. The second and third choices should be marked.
5. 31 nickels

Friday
Max Rodriguez went to New York by train.
Angela Carlson went to Wyoming by car.
Veronica Tseu went to Florida by plane.
Mitch Medina went to Hawaii by ship.

1. Correct any mistakes or write "correct."

58.43 + 81.26 = 39.69 _____

2. Correct any mistakes or write "correct."

33 x 234 = 7,722 _____

3. Estimate what 99 x 41 will be.

_____

4. List all the factors of 18.

_____

5. Marlene is typing a report that has about 300 words. If it takes her one minute to type 25 words, about how long will it take her to type the report?

_____

---

1. 2,412 ÷ 4 = _____

2.   175
      x 41

3. Is 971 odd or even?

_____

4. If $p = 5$, then what does $p + 18$ equal?

_____

5. Charlie was collecting grasshoppers to feed to his pet snake. It takes him about 2 minutes to catch each one. If he catches 13 grasshoppers, about how long will it take him?

_____

Daily Math Practice, Grade 4 • EMC 753

Name:

1. Add a sign.

1 2 9 = 108

2. Add a sign.

1 2 3 5 = 128

3. At a party 10 people want a lemon-lime soda and 13 people want cola. What is the ratio of people wanting lemon-lime to the people wanting cola?

_____

4. Does this figure have at least one line of symmetry?

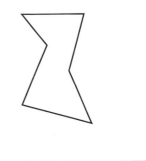

_____

5. Clarence rode a Ferris wheel 93 times around, one after the other. If each lap of the Ferris wheel took 20 seconds, how long was Clarence's ride?

_____

Name:

1. $6\overline{)1,836}$

2. 52
   x 87

3. If March 1st is on a Thursday, what day will March 20th be on?

| March | | | | | | |
Sun.	Mon.	Tues.	Wed.	Thurs.	Fri.	Sat.

_____

4. Which is heavier, 1 ton or 1 kg?

_____

5. Rachel and her sister each have saved $2.75 to buy a present for their mother. If the present costs $5.45, do they have enough money?

Why or why not? _____

_____

_____

Daily Math Practice, Grade 4 • EMC 753

Using this map, follow these directions and name the intersection where Dawn ends up.

Dawn starts at the intersection of Delaware St. and 3rd Avenue. She walks 2 blocks north, 1 block east, 4 blocks south, and turns right. She goes 2 blocks and turns right before going another 1 block. Where is Dawn located?

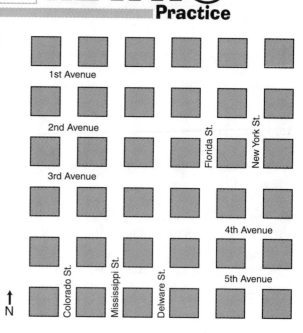

_____

Do you prefer to use right and left directions or cardinal directions (north, south, east, and west)?

_____

Why?

_____

_____

Answer Key

MATH 34
Practice

Monday

1. 58.43 + 81.26 = 139.69
2. correct
3. There are many possible answers, including 4,000 (100 x 40).
4. 1, 2, 3, 6, 9, and 18
5. about 12 minutes

Tuesday

1. 603
2. 7,175
3. odd
4. 23
5. about 26 minutes

Wednesday

1. 12 x 9 = 108
2. 123 + 5 = 128
3. 10 to 13 or 10:13
4. There is no line of symmetry.
5. 1,860 seconds or 31 minutes

Thursday

1. 306
2. 4,524
3. Tuesday
4. 1 ton
5. Yes, they have enough money because they have $5.50 and the present only costs $5.45.

Friday

She ends up at Mississippi Street and 4th Avenue.
Students' answers to the second question will vary.

1. Correct any mistakes or write "correct."

$\frac{3}{5} + \frac{1}{5} = \frac{4}{5}$ _____

2. Correct any mistakes or write "correct."

$980 + 120 = 110$ _____

3. How many feet are in 1 mile?

_____

4. How many centimeter cubes could fit inside this box?

3 cm

2 cm

5 cm

_____

5. Bryan has six dogs that each eat one-half cup of food each morning. If he has 20 cups of food, how many days can he feed all his dogs?

_____

1. $328 \div 8 =$ _____

2. $\begin{array}{r} 319 \\ \times\ 28 \\ \hline \end{array}$

3. What place value does the 5 have in 598.30?

_____

4. Which is larger, $\frac{1}{2}$ or $\frac{2}{3}$?

_____

5. Dominique was putting her CDs into her new CD racks. If each rack holds 12 CDs, how many CDs will 8 racks hold?

_____

1. Add a sign.

8   0   8 = 10

2. Add a sign.

1   5   0   3 = 450

3. Which of these figures is congruent to the first figure?

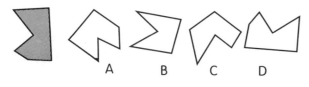

    A   B   C   D

4. If the digits 1, 2, and 3 are used once in each number, how many different three-digit numbers can be created?

_____

5. Betsy has three piles of dirty clothes in her bedroom. There are 15 pairs of pants, 12 shirts, and 8 more shirts. If the washing machine will hold only 4 shirts and 3 pairs of pants at one time, how many loads of laundry will Betsy have to do to clean all of her clothes?

_____

---

1. 7⟌4,956

2. $1\frac{2}{3}$
   $-\ \frac{3}{6}$
   ———

3. What value does **X** represent on this number line?

```
◄——|——|——|——X——|——|——|——|——|——|——►
   25          50          75
```

4. Fill in the correct symbol.

< = >

9.8 ◯ 10

5. Dee was listening to music on the radio. The radio station plays a new song about every three minutes. If Dee listens to 25 songs, about how long will she listen to the radio?

_____

Daily Math Practice, Grade 4 • EMC 753

Use the figure below to solve this problem. Where does the letter Q belong in this figure?
What about the letter M? Explain why you think they belong in those locations.

_____

_____

_____

_____

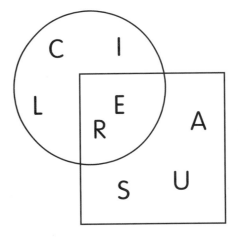

Answer Key

Monday
1. correct
2. 980 + 120 = 1,100
3. 5,280 feet
4. 30 cubic centimeters
5. 6 days (with two cups of food left over)

Tuesday
1. 41
2. 8,932
3. hundreds
4. $\frac{2}{3}$
5. 96 CDs

Wednesday
1. 80 ÷ 8 = 10
2. 150 x 3 = 450
3. D
4. 6
5. 5 loads

Thursday
1. 708
2. $\frac{7}{6}$ or $1\frac{1}{6}$
3. Students' answers may vary from 42 to 43.
4. < (less than)
5. 75 minutes or 1 hour and 15 minutes

Friday
The letter Q goes in with the S, U, and A because it is one of the letters of the word "SQUARE," but not a letter of the word "CIRCLE." The letter M goes outside the entire graph because it isn't in either word.

Daily Math Practice, Grade 4 • EMC 753

1. Correct any mistakes or write "correct."

67.2 – 38.5 = 28.7 _____

2. Correct any mistakes or write "correct."

$\frac{2}{7} + \frac{3}{7} = \frac{5}{14}$ _____

3. What is the perimeter of this figure?

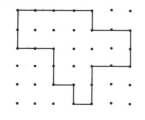

_____

4. Using the figure in problem 3, what is its area?

_____

5. Jo and Jill were baking brownies for their class party. Each batch will make 18 brownies. They want to make enough so that each student can have 2 brownies. If there are 25 people in the class, how many batches of brownies do they need to make?

_____

---

1. 6,327 ÷ 9 = _____

2.   256
      x 48
     _____

3. What are the next three numbers in this pattern?

10, 17, 24, 31, _____, _____, _____

4. 1 gallon is equal to how many cups?

_____

5. Paul went for a bike ride Saturday afternoon. If he rode 8 miles in an hour, how far did he go after riding for four hours?

_____

1. Add a sign.

1 2 8 6 3 = 65

2. Add a sign.

1 5 6 9 = 165

3. Here are three views of the same cube. What is on the side opposite the A?

_____

4. What is the probability of rolling an even number on a standard six-sided die?

_____

5. Peggy wants to buy 3 CDs that cost $14.95 each. How much will the 3 CDs cost?

_____

1. 5)4,520

2.   198
     x 57

3. What temperature is 18 degrees above 78 degrees?

_____

4. What are the first four multiples of 8?

_____

5. Howie has 27 cookies that he wants to divide evenly between himself and his four friends. How many cookies do each of them get?

_____

Use the following clues to find out what whole number goes in each region and what color it should be.

1. The sum of the regions in the oval is 15.

2. The sum of the regions in the rectangle is 9.

3. The sum of the regions in the triangle is 16.

4. The black section is 5.

5. F is blue.

6. 2 is in the green region.

7. The intersection of all three shapes is red.

8. 3 is in the A region.

9. The region that is ONLY in the oval is green.

10. E is orange.

11. One of the regions is yellow.

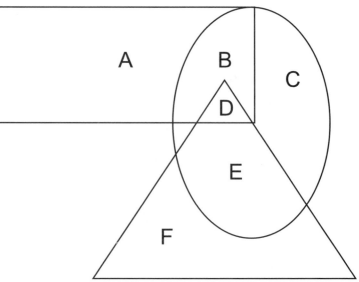

Answer Key

Monday

1. correct
2. $\frac{2}{7} + \frac{3}{7} = \frac{5}{7}$
3. 22 units
4. 17 square units
5. 3 batches

Tuesday

1. 703
2. 12,288
3. 38, 45, 52
4. 16 cups
5. 32 miles

Wednesday

1. 128 − 63 = 65
2. 156 + 9 = 165
3. F
4. 3 out of 6, 3:6, 1 out of 2, or 1:2
5. $44.85

Thursday

1. 904
2. 11,286
3. 96 degrees
4. 8, 16, 24, 32
5. $5\frac{2}{5}$ cookies each or 5.4 cookies each

Friday

A-3-yellow, B-5-black, C-2-green, D-1-red, E-7-orange, and F-8-blue